Grammar Sucks

What to Do to Make Your Writing Much More Better

Joanne Kimes
with Gary Robert Muschla

Adams Media
Avon, Massachusetts

Published by
Adams Media, an F+W Publications Company
57 Littlefield Street, Avon, MA 02322. U.S.A.
www.adamsmedia.com

ISBN 10: 1-59337-626-X
ISBN 13: 978-1-59337-626-0
Printed in the United States of America.

J I H G F E D C B A

Library of Congress Cataloging-in-Publication Data
available from the publisher

This publication is designed to provide accurate and authoritative information with regard to the subject matter covered. It is sold with the understanding that the publisher is not engaged in rendering legal, accounting,
or other professional advice. If legal advice or other expert assistance is
required, the services of a competent professional person should be sought.
— From a *Declaration of Principles* jointly adopted by a Committee of the
American Bar Association and a Committee of Publishers and Associa-
tions

Many of the designations used by manufacturers and sellers to distinguish
their product are claimed as trademarks. Where those designations appear
in this book and Adams Media was aware of a trademark claim, the designations have been printed with initial capital letters.

This book is available at quantity discounts for bulk purchases.
For information, please call 1-800-289-0963.

For my incredible daughter, Emily.
I'm so glad you happened to me.
—J.K.

For Judy and Erin, as always.
—G.R.M.

contents

acknowledgments

Thanks, Gary Muschla, the best coauthor and grammar expert ever. Without you, this would just be a book filled with silly jokes.

Thanks to Jennifer Kushnier, the best editor ever. Without *you*, this would be a book filled with misdirection.

And finally, thanks to Jeff Herman, the best agent ever. Without you there'd be no book at all. Thanks for "fixing me up" with Gary Muschla so that I could even consider doing it. We're both very grateful!

Part I

grammar lite:
or, the basics of
the english language

There's no doubt about it. Grammar sucks. It sucks big time. Sure, there are a few people out there who actually enjoy the subject, but then again, there are a few people out there who enjoy getting body piercings. These people don't really count because, well, because they scare me. But if you're anything like me, you hate grammar too. In fact, my guess is that the only reason you bought this book in the first place is that you're either in college, have an upcoming résumé to write, are forced to give a speech in front of important people, or have a school-aged child who's asking you what an irregular verb is and you haven't the faintest idea. I'd venture to say that when you walked into the bookstore, you passed by far more interesting titles than this that you would have much preferred to buy. There were epic novels and self-help books, and of course, many books written

1

by Jackie Collins. But no. You forced yourself to go into the research or reference section and buy this grammar book. Well, good news. This book may not be nearly as dull as you might have imagined it to be. In fact, instead of dry, boring facts, this grammar book is written in a casual tone and filled with jokes aplenty. In fact, you may even enjoy this book more than the other ones you wanted to buy— well, except for the ones by Jackie Collins, because those are incredibly juicy.

For your reading pleasure, this book is split into three different sections. This first section covers the fundamentals of grammar, all of which you'll need to know if you want to put a good sentence together, or at least fake it. The following sections take these principles one step further until, by the end of this book, you'll be able to speak and write like one of those boring intellectuals you despise so much! Some of the topics in this first section are quite basic and no doubt things you learned back when you thought the "s" word meant "stupid." But, although basic, all of these concepts must be grasped in order to go any further. So let's get down and dirty and get that brain in gear.

Chapter 1

the boring blocks of a sentence

Let's start with the basics. Just as a chord is the building block of a song, or a lie is the building block of a campaign speech, it's also true that a sentence is the building block of verbal and written communication. Sentences in turn are built with eight different kinds of words called the parts of speech. They are the noun, pronoun, verb, adjective, adverb, preposition, conjunction, and interjection. Since sentences are made up with these words in a specific pattern, understanding the parts of speech and their uses will help you improve both your speaking and your writing.

I know you think that you can just skip over this basic stuff, but you can't do anything without knowing the basics first. You can't drive a car without knowing what the accelerator, brake, and steering wheel are. Hell, you can't even make love without knowing the basic anatomy of the opposite sex (although men have been trying to go around this one for years). Yes, to understand anything, you need to know the basics, and grammar is no exception. So let's delve into these eight different parts of speech.

Nasty Nouns

Nouns are very important. In fact, if there were no nouns in English, none of us would have a name. For the sole use of a noun is to name things, specifically, a person, place, thing, idea, or quality. But there are several other categories of nouns that you need to know as well.

To begin with, there are *common nouns* that refer to general persons, places, things, ideas, or qualities. But since I'm calling this topic "nasty nouns," I'll use nasty words in my examples. Some examples of a common noun:

man

woman

hooker

bedroom

Next up are *proper nouns*, which refer to particular persons, places, things, ideas, organizations, institutions, months, and days. As complicated as this may seem, they're a breeze to recognize since proper nouns are always capitalized. Examples include:

Hugh Hefner

Playboy Mansion

January

Friday

Abstract nouns name a quality, an emotion, a characteristic, or an idea. Examples:

truth

goodness

beauty

Then come *concrete nouns*, which comprise things that you can build with concrete (naw, just seeing if you're still with me). Actually, concrete nouns are the names of objects that can be perceived through your senses (sight, hearing, touch, taste, and smell). Examples:

feather

leather

chocolate syrup

Count nouns nouns that can be counted. That means there can be more than one of them. When a count noun is singular and indefinite, "a" or "an" is often used with it. Examples:

tassels, a tassel

videos, a video

g-strings, a g-string

blindfolds, a blindfold

Mass nouns, also known as noncount nouns, name things that cannot be counted. Mass nouns are not used as plurals in regular English. Example:

arousal

luggage

envy

And finally, there are *collective nouns*, which name a collective group. Examples:

audience

team

class

Since sentences are about people, places, things, ideas, or qualities, nouns are the prime building blocks of all sentences. To put this all into perspective, here's an example of a sentence with the nouns italicized.

Paris Hilton drove to *Wal-Mart* to do some *shopping*.

Here's the same sentence without the nouns.

_____ drove to _____ to do some _____

As you can see, this sentence doesn't make any sense . . . but then again neither does the part about Paris Hilton shopping at a discount chain store. Although you probably don't need to know all these abstract nouns as well as Tiger Woods's handicap or every episode of *The Three Stooges*, you should know what common and proper nouns are. After all, if you want people to think you know what you're talking about, you need to know your nouns. But if you want people to think of you as the couch potato, then you really should know the other stuff about Tiger and the Three Stooges.

Pain in the Ass Pronouns

Now that you've got the noun thing down pat, let's move on to pronouns. The basic aspect of a pronoun is really quite simple. A pronoun is a word that can be substituted for a noun, whether the noun is a person, place, thing, or idea. For example: He can replace Tom; it can replace toaster. Are you with me so far? Good. The next thing to know is that the noun that the pronoun replaces is called its antecedent. Example:

Ms. Lopez explained why *she* was late to the set again.

In this sentence, the pronoun *she* refers to *Ms. Lopez*. Therefore, *Ms. Lopez* is the antecedent. (She also appears to be quite the diva, but that's beside the point.)

Unfortunately, that's not where the lesson ends (which should come as no surprise to you since you've probably noticed more words on this page). Just as there were different types of nouns, there are also different types of pronouns: personal, indefinite, demonstrative, relative, interrogative, and reflexive. Add to these categories the fact that pronouns may be singular, plural, or possessive, and that they may vary in case depending on how they are used in a sentence, and you can now fully understand why pronouns are truly a pain in the ass!

But my job is to simplify this mumbo jumbo for you, so let's see what I can do. I'm going to state each of the various types of pronouns and then attempt to explain them to you. Here's the lowdown on pronouns:

Personal Pronouns

To begin with, there is the *personal pronoun*, which refers to a particular person, place, thing, or idea. It can either be singular, plural, or possessive. Singular means that the pronoun refers to only one person, place, or thing; plural means the pronoun replaces more than one; and possessive pronouns show ownership, and would no doubt be the jealous type if you decided to date one. Here are some examples of a personal pronoun.

Singular: I, you, he, she, it, me, him, her

Plural: we, you (as in "all of you"), they, us, them

Possessive: my, mine, your, yours, his, her, hers, its, our, ours, their, theirs

Indefinite Pronouns

Then there are *indefinite pronouns*, which refer to nonspecific persons, places, or things. These types of pronouns don't require an antecedent. They can be singular or plural, and sometimes can even swing both ways. Just think of indefinite pronouns as the bisexuals of the English language.

Singular: another, anybody, each, either, everyone, everything, much, neither, no one, nothing, one, other, somebody, someone, something

Plural: both, few, many, others, several

Singular or Plural: all, any, more, most, none, some

Demonstrative Pronouns

Next up, *demonstrative pronouns*, which are very touchy feely and point directly to their antecedents.

Singular: this, that

Plural: these, those

Relative Pronouns

Then come *relative pronouns*, which are used to introduce dependent clauses, including:

who, whom, which, what, that, whose, whoever, whichever, whatever

Interrogative Pronouns

Interrogative pronouns are used in questions. Notice that interrogative pronouns are quite similar to relative pronouns:

who, whom, which, what, whose

Example: *Whose* cell phone is this?

Reflexive and Intensive Pronouns

And finally, there are *reflexive* and *intensive pronouns*, which are personal pronouns that are combined with the term *self* or *selves*.

Singular: myself, yourself, himself, herself, itself

Plural: ourselves, yourselves, themselves

Example (reflexive): George reminded *himself* to go to the grocery store on his way home from work or else he'd get no lovin' tonight.

Example (intensive): Susan *herself* is always grateful to George when he does what he's been told.

There! We're done! Get up and stretch and take a relaxing cleansing breath. We've gone over everything you've always wanted to know about pronouns but were afraid to ask! You are officially qualified to tell someone that you went to the mall: *I* went to the mall. Congratulations!

But, like all frustrating aspects of grammar, things tend to get confusing. Many pronouns, like *her*, for example, and *who* and *whom* (the duo responsible for more confusion than what nearsighted and farsighted actually mean) are in more than one category. Then comes another infuriating aspect to it all, which is when pronouns are referred to according to case—subjective, objective, or possessive—which depends on the way that they're used in a sentence. Like I warned, pronouns can be a pain in the ass, and we'll discuss more things in detail, like possessives, in part 2 of this book. That is, if you can hang in there that long. I realize this stuff may be confusing and that you may want to lay down, forget about grammar and speak real bad forever. But if you didn't notice anything wrong with that last sentence, I suggest that you stick with it a bit longer.

Very Vexing Verbs

Now that we've learned a thing or twelve about nouns and pronouns, let's move on to the part of the sentence where all the action takes place: namely, verbs. Unlike nouns, verbs aren't as clear-cut to understand as a simple "person, place, or thing." In fact, there are more variations of verbs than there are ways to spend money on eBay. Just as hunger pangs make dieting hard, the many forms of verbs make grammar hard. The way I see it, if it weren't for verbs, understanding grammar would be a heck of a lot easier. So take off your coat and stay awhile because it's time for me to give you the lowdown on verbs.

Technically, a verb is a word that expresses an action or a state of being. *Action verbs* show something happening, while a state-of-being verb (commonly called a *linking verb*) describes the condition or state of some person or thing. Here are a couple examples of action verbs so that you can better understand just what the heck I'm talking about:

Dustin *walked* to Pink's for a hot dog.
Angelina *waved* and *smiled* at Cher at The Ivy.

Here are examples of linking, or state-of-being, verbs:

Liam *is* taller in person.
Meryl *seemed* uneasy at the Oscars.

I'm sure with the examples above you've learned the difference between action verbs and linking verbs. You've also no doubt learned that I'm quite obsessed with Hollywood gossip. As you can imagine, the vast majority of verbs are actually action verbs. But interestingly enough, the typical linking verb is used far more often than the typical action verb. Some of the most common linking verbs are words like *appear, be, become, feel, grow, look, remain, seem, smell, sound, stay,* and *taste.* To complicate matters further, each of these verbs has various parts. For instance, the forms of the verb *to be* include: *am, are, is, was, were, be,* and *being,* as well as all verb phrases ending in either *been* or *be,* like *have been, could have been,* and *should be.* See, I can already see your eyebrows furrowing together and I'm just getting started! As you are probably realizing, verbs can most definitely suck!

In most cases, it's quite clear as to whether a verb is an action verb or a linking verb. But of course, there are several instances where that may not be the case. Don't you hate this part about grammar? We spend all this time learning about a certain rule, and then we find out that oftentimes, the rule is no longer true. If only traffic rules were as forgiving as grammar rules, I wouldn't get a thank-you card from the police department for all the income I generate!

When it comes to verbs, there are those that can either express action or be linking verbs, depending on their use in a sentence. Check this out to get a better idea of what I mean:

> The flower *smelled* sweet. (linking)
> Jan *smelled* the flower. (action)
> The cake *tasted* awful. (linking)
> Peter *tasted* the cake. (action)

Unlike the other hellish grammar rules that you simply have to memorize, I'm going to show you an easy trick to grasping this one. Basically, a simple test to determine whether a verb is a linking verb is to substitute *is* or *was* for it. Consider the first example. The flower *smelled* sweet.

The flower *was* sweet. Since *was* can replace *smelled*, *smelled* in this sentence is a linking verb. But consider the second example. Jan *smelled* the flower. Substitute *was* for *smelled* and you get, Jan *was* the flower. Unless Jan was ten and in some school play about photosynthesis, *smelled* would be an action verb.

When attempting to understand verbs, simply knowing whether they express action or link a subject of a sentence with the word following the verb isn't enough. There are several other things to know, like the names of the various verbs (yes, it just keeps getting worse and worse now, doesn't it?).

Verb Phrases

Let's start with the *verb phrase*. A verb phrase functions as a verb in a sentence and is made up of a main verb and at least one helping verb. In a verb phrase, the helping verb does precisely what its name implies—it helps the main verb. Now, don't start to tremble. I'm going to give you an example to make all this stuff clear. A good example of a verb phrase is *has called*. *Called* is the main verb, because it expresses the action, and *has* is the helping verb. Common helping verbs include the forms of the verbs *be*, *have*, and *do*, as well as the verbs *may*, *might*, *can*, *could*, *will*, *would*, *shall*, *should*, and *must*.

Transitive and Intransitive Verbs

Another important thing to know is that verbs can also be *transitive* or *intransitive*. It may seem like a minor thing, but the prefix *in* makes all the difference. A transitive verb requires an object to complete its meaning. For example: Lindsay Lohan caught the movie (sorry, I can't just stop my obsession like that, you know). *Movie* completes the meaning of the verb *caught*. Obviously, without *movie* to complete

❝I always thought that a transitive verb was called a 'transient' verb and that it was a group of verbs that were about homeless people. Then again, I always thought that Def Leppard was a singer who was deaf!**❞**

—Jennifer

the sentence, *caught* doesn't have much meaning. What did Lindsay catch? A cold? A fish? A disease from the toilet seat in one of those sleazy nightclubs that she hangs out at until far too late?

Unlike a transitive verb, an intransitive verb expresses complete action without an object.

Example: Each morning, Goldie *jogs*.

In this sentence, *jogs* expresses the complete action without the need of any other words. Goldie jogs. Okay, you get a clear mental picture of a perky woman jogging along a road with a team of paparazzi trailing behind her hoping she'll fall flat on her ass so they can sell the photo for people like me to gawk at.

Depending on their use in a sentence, many verbs can function transitively or intransitively. In the following sentences, see if you can tell which is the example of the transitive verb and which is the intransitive verb (I bet you didn't think there'd be a pop quiz now, did you? Don't worry, though; it won't go on your permanent record).

Seeing the microphone, he *ran*.

He *ran* the show.

If you guessed the first one is the intransitive verb, you'd be right. The second example is the transitive verb. If you missed that one, you need to stay after school and clean all the erasers.

If you need some help remembering the difference between transitive and intransitive verbs, just remember that, just as a transitive verb needs an object to define its meaning, a transsexual needs a certain genital-like object to define his or her meaning, as well.

Moving on, you also need to know that verbs can either be *regular* or *irregular*. Regular verbs form their past tense and past participle (see below) by adding *d* or *ed* to the present form. Irregular verbs don't. They form their past and past participles irregularly—there is no particular rule. Examples:

Catch, caught (irregular)
Talk, talked (regular)

There are four different principal parts that are associated with verbs. These parts are the present tense, the past tense, the past participle, and the present participle. The principal parts of verbs are designed to tell the time of an action or state of being. In the example below notice how the participle forms require helping verbs. The past participle requires the helping verbs *have*, *has*, or *had*; the present participle requires a form of the verb *to be* (*am*, *is*, *was*, *are*, *were*, as well as phrases ending in *been* or *be*).

Present	Past	Past Participle	Present Participle
call	called	(have) called	(am) calling
walk	walked	(have) walked	(am) walking
cry	cried	(have) cried	(am) crying

Present	Past	Past Participle	Present Participle
begin	began	(have) begun	(am) beginning
do	did	(have) done	(am) doing
catch	caught	(have) caught	(am) catching

As you can see, there isn't any pattern for forming the past participles in the irregular verbs like *begin* and *do*. And, as you can also see, the example words are really quite dull. I tried to make them funny, but you try packing a whole lotta humor into only one single word!

I know it sounds like a lot of information to swallow, but at least we've gone over the basics. You know that verbs show action or a state of being. You know that they're essential to a sentence. And you know that I really get a lot of use out of my subscription to *Star* magazine.

Annoying Adjectives

Adjectives are descriptive words that are used to modify a noun or pronoun. If they're used sparingly and specifically, they can make the meaning of a noun or pronoun more definite and precise. But if they're used to extreme and exuberance—as too many people do—they are just plain annoying. And since there are so many other things in life that are annoying, the least you can do is limit the amount of bothersome adjectives.

Adjectives may modify nouns or pronouns in any of three ways:

The adjective tells what kind: *staticky* reception, *frozen* computer, *stuck* zipper.

The adjective tells which one: *this* busy signal, *those* traffic jams.

The adjective tells how many: *four* mosquito bites, *several* gray hairs, *many* problems.

In most instances, adjectives come before the noun or pronoun they modify. It isn't unusual, though, for an adjective to follow the word it modifies. Here's an example: The molars, *painful* and *impacted*, must be extracted right away.

Predicate Adjectives

A special kind of adjective is known as the predicate adjective. This adjective is separated from the noun or pronoun it modifies by a verb. Predicate adjectives follow linking verbs. Example: My date is *boring*. *Boring* modifies *my date*.

Determiners

We also have adjectives called determiners that serve a special function in a sentence. Their big job is to introduce nouns and noun phrases. Following are examples of determiners:

The articles: the, a, an (example: *the* sky)

Possessive adjectives: his, her, its, your, our, their (example: *her* gloves)

Interrogative adjectives: whose, which, what (example: *Whose* keys?)

Demonstrative adjectives: this, that, these, those (example: *those* books)

Indefinite adjectives: all, any, both, each, every, few, many, several, some (example: *several* books)

Along with lacking comparative or superlative forms, determiners don't serve as predicate adjectives, and they aren't used in combination with other adjectives. Note that many of these words can also serve as pronouns, depending on the way they are used in a sentence. Check these examples:

Teresa always misplaces *her* car keys. (possessive adjective)

The tax audit letter was addressed to *her*. (objective pronoun)

These examples illustrate one of the most confusing aspects of English and grammar and are the ones that are the most likely to make you pound your head into the wall in frustration. Many words have different meanings based on the way they are used in a sentence.

Understanding that adjectives are descriptive words that modify nouns and pronouns is just the beginning, however. There are even more bothersome, yet important, things to learn about them in part 2. Are they any less annoying, you may ask? Well, if you think about the title of this book, you can answer that question yourself. Until that time, let's turn our attention to adverbs.

The Trouble with Adverbs

Adverbs are words that modify verbs, adjectives, other adverbs, clauses, or sentences. They're different from adjectives in that adjectives only modify nouns and pronouns. Adverbs can heighten or sharpen the meaning of words they modify. But, like adjectives, overusing them in speaking or writing can make you sound like a *totally*, *completely*, and *hopelessly* inept communicator of our *wonderfully*, *richly*, and *marvelously* expressive English language today, tomorrow, and beyond (you guessed it, the adverbs are in italics).

The key to using adverbs effectively is to use them sparingly, just like visiting your in-laws. Adverbs are used when necessary to answer one of the following questions in a sentence:

How? Cory works *hard. Hard* tells how he works, which explains why he needs time off.

When? Cory and his wife, Jen, plan their vacation *now. Now* tells when they plan their vacation.

Where? Jen wants to go *there. There* tells where Jen wants to go, which just happens to be where her parents live.

How often? A plane departs *hourly. Hourly* tells how often a plane departs to Cory's in-laws.

To what extent? The last time they went there, it *nearly* ended their marriage. *Nearly* tells how close Cory and Jen came to divorcing.

Along with answering the above questions, adverbs are often used to start a question. Four common adverbs used in this way are *how*, *when*, *where*, and *why*.

How did Jen convince Cory to go?

Where did Cory want to go?

When will Cory finally be able to take his dream vacation to the annual bacon festival?

Why is it that Cory just bought a new pair of ear plugs?

Many adverbs can be recognized by their ending in *–ly*. In fact, most adverbs are formed by adding –ly to an adjective. Note the following:

brightly	freshly	softly
broadly	gracefully	strongly
calmly	hopefully	successfully
clearly	narrowly	sweetly
completely	quickly	tenderly

deeply	richly	tightly
dryly	roughly	warmly
eagerly	sternly	widely

Obviously, there are many more. Some adverbs, however, don't end in –ly, as shown in the following list:

almost	just	still
already	maybe	then
also	never	therefore
always	often	today
ever	seldom	tomorrow
forever	so	very
here	soon	yet

Note that some adverbs, like so many words in English, can serve as different parts of speech depending on the way they are used in a sentence. *Today* and *tomorrow*, which often serve as nouns, are good examples.

Cory and Jen leave *today*.

In this sentence *today* tells when Cory and Jen are leaving and is an adverb.

Unlike adjectives that generally come before the noun or pronoun they modify, adverbs enjoy a variety of positions in a sentence, depending on the kind of adverb and the construction of the sentence. When modifying a verb, they may come before the verb, after the verb, or may even separate the parts of a verb phrase. In many cases the position is a result of a person's individual speaking or writing style. Note the examples:

Soon Cory will want to punch out his mother-in-law.

Cory will want to punch out his mother-in-law *soon*.

Cory will *soon* want to punch out his mother-in-law.

When modifying an adjective or another adverb, an adverb usually comes directly before the word it modifies. Here is an example of an adverb modifying an adjective.

His mother-in-law considers herself to be a *totally* honest woman, and doesn't hesitate to call Cory a loser.

Totally modifies the adjective *honest*. If you were to place *totally* anywhere else, the sentence would lose clarity, and you too would be called a loser by Jen's mom.

This also holds true for an adverb that modifies another adverb.

Cory works *extremely carefully* to avoid her.

The example above is clear in its meaning. These are not:

Extremely, Cory works carefully to avoid her.

Cory extremely works carefully to avoid her.

Cory works carefully extremely to avoid her.

When used effectively, adverbs can help you communicate ideas clearly. But an important lesson to learn is that when not used effectively, they make communication cumbersome. Cory also learns an important lesson: if he and Jen were to ever divorce, his next wife has to be an orphan.

Now you know the basics about adverbs. Note that I said the "basics." There's much more about adverbs and their proper use in part 2 when we get into the trickier stuff.

Puzzling Prepositions

There are many rules in life. Don't covet thy neighbor's wife. Don't run with scissors. And, of course, don't end a sentence with a preposition. But unless you know what a preposition is, you may have committed this last sin hundreds of times and didn't even know it. The way I always remembered it from school—a preposition is a word that can describe the ways a pen can be near to a table. It can be in it, on it, under it, beyond it, etc. But as it turns out, there's much more to the story.

Technically, a preposition is a word that shows the relationship of a noun or a pronoun to some other word in a sentence. Prepositions come before nouns, pronouns, and their modifiers (page 41) to form prepositional phrases. The noun or pronoun in a prepositional phrase is called the object of the preposition. After reading this paragraph, you now understand why I only remembered the pen explanation. It's much easier to follow.

When speaking or writing, most people don't think much about prepositions. Instead, they focus on nouns and verbs, which are the key players of sentences. Yet, prepositions are also very important. Okay, maybe not as important as backing up your computer or having a decent anti-frizz hair product, but prepositions do carry their weight in grammar. Prepositions and their resulting phrases allow speakers and writers to embellish their sentences with information. Here's an example of what I mean:

Jimmy watched football *on a big screen TV.*

On a big screen TV is a prepositional phrase. *On* is the preposition, and *TV*, which is a noun, is the object of the preposition. (The words *a*, *big*, and *screen* modify the noun *TV*.)

Notice that although *Jimmy watched football* is a complete sentence, the prepositional phrase adds a lot of information. Jimmy doesn't merely watch football on the old black and white set that he keeps in the spare bedroom because he really doesn't like house guests. Instead, he watches on a big screen TV, which is why he is the envy of all his friends (and maybe the reason why people like to stay over at his house in the first place).

The following are some common prepositions so that you can better recognize them and therefore know not to end a sentence with them:

aboard	beside	into	to
about	between	near	toward
above	beyond	of	under
across	by	off	underneath
after	despite	on	until
against	down	onto	unto
along	during	out	up
around	except	outside	upon
at	for	over	with
before	from	past	within
below	in	through	without

Sometimes prepositions appear in combinations, for example: *along with, in front of, in spite of, on account of,* or *together with.*

Prepositions can also be combined with some verbs to form *phrasal verbs* (now why couldn't they have just called them prepositional verbs? I'm convinced our forefathers of grammar had a wicked sense of humor). Some examples of phrasal verbs include: *do without*, *put up with*, *look past*, and *look over*. In a phrasal verb the preposition is called a *particle*. Note the following example:

> Serena *looked past* her earlier defeat and rallied to win the championship.

"Looked past" is a phrasal verb with "past" as the particle. The phrase means that Serena was able to ignore her earlier defeat. Notice that the following sentence doesn't contain a phrasal verb:

> Serena looked *past the net* at her opponent.
>
> *Past the net* is a prepositional phrase. *Past* is the preposition and *net* is the object.

Prepositions are good for enhancing simple sentences and relating words to each other. Understanding prepositions and prepositional phrases is puzzling, but it's also necessary if you're going to be a stickler for grammar and never end a sentence with one. Also necessary is keeping that anti-frizz hair product with you at all times on really humid days.

Catchy Conjunctions

Conjunctions have always been a breeze for me to understand since I was lucky enough to grow up when *Schoolhouse Rock* played on TV. If you were too, then you're familiar with the famous question, "Conjunction Junction, what's your function?" You can see those little trains hookin' up words in boxcars and can hear that catchy theme song that lingers in your head like a stubborn sinus headache. But if you're too young or, heaven forbid, have parents who didn't let you watch TV because they thought the rays were bad for your eyes (as they did in those earlier years), then let me explain.

Conjunctions are connecting words that can join together two sentences, clauses, phrases, or words. Whether you realize it or not, you use the three types of conjunctions many times a day: coordinating conjunctions, correlative conjunctions, and subordinating conjunctions.

Coordinating conjunctions connect sentences, clauses, phrases, and words that are similar in some way and have the same grammatical form. Examples of coordinating conjunctions include: *and, but, or, nor, for, so,* and *yet.* Note the following examples:

> **Connecting two sentences:** My parents wouldn't let me watch TV as a kid, *but* they would let me eat chemical-ridden bologna sandwiches for lunch every day.
>
> **Connecting two clauses:** If I were to put my Hot Wheels away *and* if I were to clean my room, I'd be able to have Jello 1-2-3 for dessert.
>
> **Connecting two phrases:** I played with my Clackers *and* with my Atari game.
>
> **Connecting two words:** Billy *and* Stevie had the same Weebles characters as I did.

When a coordinating conjunction connects two sentences, as in the first example, a comma generally follows the first sentence and precedes the conjunction. The comma shows that the sentences are equal in importance and that they can stand alone.

Continuing down memory lane with the use of conjunctions, we come to *correlative conjunctions,* which are pairs of words that serve as connectors. There are several pairs: *either . . . or, neither . . . nor, both . . . and, whether . . . or, not only . . . but also.* Correlative conjunctions join words or groups of words and add emphasis to the parts of a sentence they join. Here are some examples:

Connecting words: When I rode with my parents when I was a kid, I used neither seatbelts nor booster seats.

Connecting groups of words: When I used Gee Your Hair Smells Terrific shampoo, it not only washed my hair but also really did make it smell quite terrific.

Finally, there are *subordinating conjunctions*, which introduce dependent clauses and connect them to main clauses. A main clause expresses a complete thought and can stand alone as a sentence. Although a dependent clause has a subject and verb, it does not express a complete thought and can't stand alone. It is "dependent" on being attached to a main clause.

Several words and some phrases are used as subordinating conjunctions. The most common appear below:

after	how	unless
although	if	until
as	inasmuch as	when
as if	since	whenever
as long as	so that	where
because	than	wherever
before	till	while

Here are a few subordinating conjunctions in action:

If you were willing to spend a whole dime, you could buy a candy bar.

Although we had no remote controls, we could still change the channel by actually getting off our butts and walking over to the set to turn the knob.

Yes, without the convenience of conjunctions we would all speak and write in much simpler sentences. And although when I was a kid, it was a much simpler time, it still had its share of problems. Like when those glass Clackers broke right in front of my face and nearly blinded me, and when my mom stopped fast and I was almost thrown out of the car. I guess that now the world may not be as simple, but it sure is a heck of a lot safer! At least some of the time.

Not-So-Interesting Interjections

I find nothing in grammar to be very interesting, and interjections are no exception to this rule. But at least they're a concept that's relatively easy to grasp. In sum, interjections are words or sounds that express emotion. They don't have any grammatical relation to other words in a sentence; they're just used to add a little flavor and spice.

The list of interjections sounds more like words from a porn movie script than words from the English language, for just about any word or utterance can serve as an interjection. Here's a list of some of the most common interjections, which, coincidently, is the exact same dialog from the classic film, *Debbie Does Dallas*:

ah	oh	ugh
aha	oh no	well
help	ooh	wow
hey	ouch	yeah

Depending on the degree of the emotion that's expressed, an interjection is followed by an exclamation point or a comma. Great emotion, of course, requires the exclamation; lesser emotion requires a comma. Here are some examples:

> Ah, here comes the pizza delivery boy.
>
> Ugh, his muscles are so big.
>
> Ouch! Watch where you put that melted cheese, Buddy!

Interjections have their uses, but you need to exert caution. Peppering your conversation or writing with interjections will make you seem at the least hyperactive, or at the worst an overly bubbly teenager. Because of this, interjections should be used only when necessary (unless of course you're writing for the sequel: *Debbie Does Dallas Again*).

There, we did it! We're done talking about the Boring Blocks of a Sentence!

Chapter 2

putting all the crap together

Now that you've learned all the various types of words in the English language, we're going to take the next step and learn how to string them all together. To begin with, words can be combined to form clauses and phrases, which are the substance of sentences. They're like the meat in a meatloaf, or the soap in a soap opera. But before you can gain a complete understanding of how sentences are constructed, you need to understand how words are arranged to form them.

Clauses and Phrases—Not Just Groups of Words

A clause is more than just the wrong spelling of a jolly old man with a bowlful of jelly. It's also a group of words that contains a subject and a predicate. The subject of a clause is a noun. Remember, that's a person, place, thing, or idea about which something is said. The predicate says something about the subject. Don't worry too much about them now because they're the first things you're going to learn in part 2, when we kick things up a notch. But for now, here's an example:

Jane loves her cell phone.

The subject is *Jane* and the predicate is *loves her cell phone*.

Now that you know what a clause is, you should know that there are two kinds of them. I like to refer to them as the husband and wife of clauses. There's the *independent* clause (also called a *main* clause), which acts more like the wife. She's strong and confident, expresses a complete thought, and can stand alone as a sentence. A *dependent* clause (also called a *subordinate* clause) acts more like the husband and relies on the wife for doing his laundry and his cooking and picking up his dirty underwear off the bathroom floor. A dependent clause doesn't express a complete thought and therefore can't stand alone as a sentence. Dependent clauses always function as a part of a sentence and must be attached at the hip to the wife in order for the sentence to make any sense at all. Note the clauses in the following example:

The husband wanted to go to a strip joint, but his wife said no.

This sentence contains two independent clauses connected by the conjunction *but*. Each clause can stand alone as a sentence.

The husband wanted to go to a strip joint.
His wife said no.

Now consider this sentence:

Although the husband wanted to go to the strip joint, his wife said no.

This sentence contains the dependent clause *Although the husband wanted to go to the strip joint,* followed by the independent clause *his wife said no.* By itself, the first clause doesn't make sense and therefore can't stand alone. But the second one can. The dependent clause doesn't express a complete thought even though it contains a subject (*the husband*) and predicate (*wanted to go to the strip joint*). The independent clause is necessary for the sentence to make sense . . . and of course to do all the housework and the cooking and the shopping.

There are three kinds of dependent clauses: *adjective* clauses, *adverb* clauses, and *noun* clauses. Adjective clauses (also called *relative* clauses) modify nouns or pronouns; adverb clauses modify verbs, adjectives, adverbs, or other clauses; and noun clauses are used as nouns in a sentence. These dependent clauses will be discussed in detail in part 3, so even though you don't have to worry your pretty little head about them now, here are three examples:

> **Adjective clause:** The actor *who can't remember his lines* won't be an actor for long. The clause modifies the noun *actor.*
>
> **Adverb clause:** *As soon as we left,* the snow started. The clause modifies the verb *started.*
>
> **Noun clause:** *Whoever took that picture* will be rich. The clause functions as the subject of the sentence.

Now that we're done chatting about clauses, it's time to move on to phrases. Just as there are different kinds of clauses, there are also different kinds of phrases. To be specific, a phrase is a group of related words used as a part of speech. Phrases can't stand alone as sentences. Phrases add details to sentences and are generally broken down into four major types: *prepositional* phrases, *participial* phrases, *gerund* phrases, and *infinitive* phrases. These in turn can be broken down into even more subtypes, all of which are explained in part 3. For now, simply knowing that phrases are groups of related words that embellish sentences with details is enough to get you through this first part of this book without stress.

Clauses and phrases are specific arrangements of words that play important roles in constructing good sentences. They're not just groups of words tossed together in some haphazard manner like dice on a craps table. A lack of understanding of clauses and phrases can lead to problems in writing. And a desire to frequent strip clubs can lead to problems in a marriage.

Serious Sentence Types

If you think of a word as an individual piece of Lego, then think of a sentence as a cute little sculpture your kid makes out of Legos while you frantically try to get dinner ready before he gets bored. But what exactly makes up a sentence, and how do you know if it's complete?

The cardinal rule for a complete sentence is that it contains a *subject* and a *predicate* and expresses a complete thought. A subject is a noun or pronoun, and a predicate is a verb or verb phrase. The subject of a sentence is the part of the sentence about which something is being said. The predicate is the part of a sentence that says something about the subject. Here's an example that's consistent with the classic toy theme:

Maria runs to Target to buy Lincoln Logs for her kid.

In this example *Maria* is the subject; *runs to Target to buy Lincoln Logs for her kid* is the predicate.

Sentences can be classified according to their purpose or their structure. Whatever its purpose or structure, however, every complete sentence must have a subject and a predicate.

Although there are infinite possibilities of what a sentence can be, there are actually only four reasons for a sentence. They can make a statement, ask a question, give an order, or express some kind of great emotion. Here are some more details of what I mean:

A *declarative sentence* makes a statement and is followed by a period.

Example: The LIncoln Log gave Billy a nasty splinter.

An *interrogative sentence* asks a question and is followed by a question mark.

Example: How big was the splinter?

An *exclamatory sentence* expresses great emotion and is followed by an exclamation point.

Example: It's huge! Gigantic!

An *imperative sentence* is a command or order and is followed by a period.

Example: Get me the chain saw.

Sentences may also be classified according to their structure: simple, compound, complex, and compound-complex:

A *simple sentence* has one independent clause and no dependent clauses. (Have you seriously forgotten already? Get thee back to Chapter 1!)

Example: Jane plays with Gumby every day.

A *compound sentence* contains two or more independent clauses. The independent clauses are often connected by a comma and a coordinating conjunction (*and, but, or, nor, for, so,* or *yet*).

Example: Jane likes the pointy head of Gumby, but Lisa prefers the cute orange color of Pokey.

A *complex sentence* contains one independent clause and one or more dependent clauses connected by a subordinating conjunction (some examples being *although, as, because, when,* and *while*).

Example: Although the two kids tried to decide which toy was better, they couldn't come to an agreement. (The independent clause is *they couldn't come to an agreement.* The dependent clause is *Although the two kids tried to decide which toy was better.*)

A *compound-complex sentence* has two or more independent clauses and one or more dependent clauses.

Example: Because they couldn't decide, their mom took both toys away, and now the kids are stuck playing with rocks. (The independent clauses are *their mom took both toys away* and *now the kids are stuck playing with rocks.* The dependent clause is *Because they couldn't decide.*)

Now that you know about the different kinds of sentences, you're much better equipped to write and speak in grammatically correct sentences. And now that you know the outcome of not agreeing on rubberized nostalgic toys, you have far less chance of being stuck playing with rocks.

Frazzled Fragments

Fragments are actually incomplete sentences. They're part of a sentence that doesn't express a complete thought. People speak in fragments in everyday conversation all the time, but in formal speaking or writing, fragments are a sign that someone doesn't care much for grammar, or doesn't know much about grammar.

By definition, fragments are called "fragments" because they are grammatically incomplete sentences. They may lack a subject, or a predicate, or both. Since a subject and a predicate are necessary to express a complete thought, a fragment missing one of these essential parts at best expresses half of a thought. From the perspective of the educated, a half-thought might equal a half-wit.

Here is an example of a fragment:

Michael Jackson's nose can double as a coat hook. And a deli slicer.

Although *And a deli slicer* starts with a capital letter and ends with a period, the words only make a phrase. They don't express a complete thought. They don't have a subject or a predicate and by themselves are quite confusing, as is the reason why Michael would do such a horrendous thing to his nose in the first place.

Here's another example:

When Mike Brady wasn't looking. Alice would make goo-goo eyes at him.

The opening clause is a fragment. It begins the sentence but then needs more to finish the complete thought. It is grammatically incomplete. *When Mike Brady wasn't looking . . .* Okay, what happened next? Did Marsha steal Jan's thunder again? Did Carol get another dorky haircut? Or did it suddenly become clear why two separate families can join together so easily without any of the kids ever saying, "You can't make me! You're not my real parent!"?

The examples are clear: Fragments are not sentences. So, why do people speak in fragments? Sometimes people speak and write the way they think. And since a lot of us grew up watching way too many MTV videos, we tend to think in short chunks of information, and we express our thoughts as fragments. Of course, sometimes it's plain old laziness. Why bother to finish a thought when people will probably understand what you're trying to say anyhow? Then there are those completely frazzled people, who, due to believing lies like women can have it all, are forced to be wife, mother, cook, cleaner, and career woman all at the same time, so we don't have the time or energy to communicate in complete thoughts, let alone pay the bills or feed the dog . . . hey, where was I? Oh yeah, frazzled fragments.

The two points that come from this are obvious. One, husbands need to do more around the house. And two, if you want to come across as knowledgeable about grammar, professional on the job, and at least minimally educated in social circles, you must speak and write in complete sentences.

Fortunately, this is not as hard to do as it may sound, and a heck of a lot easier than getting your husband to throw in a load of whites. To avoid speaking and writing in fragments, make sure every sentence has a subject and predicate and that it expresses a complete thought. To find fragments in your writing, read every sentence to make sure it expresses a complete thought. If it doesn't, it's a fragment. To correct fragments, combine fragments with a sentence or with another fragment so that a complete thought results.

66 I like to think of myself as a creative person and I like to think of my writing style as artistic too. I know that I use a lot of fragments but I see it as an outlet for my creativity. Unfortunately, my boss doesn't quite see it that way, and he's forbidden me from sending out any more company memos. **99**

—Gary

Using the examples already noted, it's quite easy:

Michael Jackson's nose can double as a coat hook and a deli slicer.
When Mike Brady wasn't looking, Alice would make goo-goo eyes at him.

Avoiding and fixing fragments isn't hard. All it takes is a little concentration. And the reward for your effort is significant, because people will figure you know your grammar, or at least you know enough not to speak or write in fragments. If only fixing your life was that easy!

Run-On Sentences That Keep On Running

A run-on sentence is the Montezuma's Revenge of grammar, for just like the bowels of someone with this nasty gastrointestinal affliction, run-on sentences just keep on going and going. The typical run-on sentence occurs when two or more independent clauses are combined without a conjunction or any punctuation. Montezuma's Revenge, on the other hand, occurs when you stay at cheap hotels when traveling south of the border. Here's an example of a run-on sentence:

Jill left for Tijuana early she wanted to load up on nicotine withdrawal
pills that she could buy over the counter.

The first independent clause is *Jill left for Tijuana early*.
The second is *she wanted to load up on nicotine withdrawal pills
that she could buy over the counter*. Both are complete sentences
and need to either be connected with a subordinating conjunction (such as *because*) or separated into the two complete
sentences that they are. Here's another example:

Jill found a pharmacy she went inside.

In this example, the two independent clauses are *Jill
found a pharmacy* and *she went inside*. Again, each is a separate
sentence and should either be separated or put in a room
until they make nice.

Another type of run-on occurs when a comma connects
two independent clauses without a coordinating conjunction. This is sometimes called a comma splice. Note the
example:

She bought the pills, she headed for home.

Although run-on sentences with comma splices are used
in casual conversation, they aren't acceptable in written or
formal English with the exception of occasional short, parallel sentences. Here are some more examples:

Some days are good, some days are bad.
The cup's half full, the cup's half empty.
Day follows night, night follows day.

Note that although the above examples are generally
acceptable, you should not overuse them. In written English, especially when standard conventions are expected, it's

a safer bet to insert a conjunction: *Some days are good, and some days are bad.*

Now that you know what a run-on sentence is, you might be wondering what causes run-ons. Run-on sentences are often the result of fast thinking, fast speaking, and fast writing. As we gallop along with our ideas, we string thoughts together and skip punctuation. Of course, run-ons can also be caused by an abysmal lack of understanding of sentence structure and punctuation, but hopefully we're beyond that since we're already halfway through part 1. In the end, your boss won't really care why the last report you handed in was sprinkled with run-ons. He'll only care that your sloppy writing and thinking style isn't what he's looking for in a partner.

Fortunately, run-on sentences are easy to avoid by clarifying your ideas and recognizing when one complete thought ends and another begins. In speaking, expressing your ideas in complete thoughts generally eliminates most run-ons. As for writing, while it's certainly better not to make mistakes with run-ons in the first place, you can catch them through careful proofreading of your work. Examine each sentence. If each of the parts of a sentence can stand alone, the sentence might be a run-on. As you proofread your written work, pay attention to places you naturally pause. Pauses can be clues that indicate where punctuation is needed. If you pause in the midst of a sentence where there is no punctuation, the sentence might be a run-on. If you pause for a comma, make sure that the comma is not joining two independent clauses without the help of a coordinating conjunction.

Correcting Run-Ons

Once you've identified a run-on sentence, you have several options for how to correct it. The first and easiest method is to insert a period, which will separate the two independent clauses. Note the examples:

> Jill is a woman with nicotine fits and the runs she wishes that she were dead. (run-on)

> Jill is a woman with nicotine fits and the runs, she wishes that she were dead. (run-on)

> Jill is a woman with nicotine fits and the runs. She wishes that she were dead. (correct)

Be careful with this method, however, because it can lead to short sentences that make writing and speaking choppy.

Another method for correcting run-ons is to add a comma (if necessary) and a coordinating conjunction (*and*, *or*, *but*, *nor*, *for*, or *yet*). Note the correct example:

> Jill is a woman with nicotine fits and the runs, and she wishes that she were dead.

Yet another method for correction is to separate the clauses with a semicolon. This method is best used if two parts of a run-on are of relatively equal importance, as the example shows:

> Jill is a woman with nicotine fits and the runs; she wishes that she were dead.

A final method for correction is to rewrite one clause as a dependent clause, using a subordinating conjunction (for example, *although*, *because*, *if*, or *while*) or a relative pronoun (for example, *that*, *which*, or *who*). Note the examples:

> Jill is a woman with nicotine fits and the runs who wishes that she were dead.

> Because Jill is a woman with nicotine fits and the runs, she wishes that she were dead.

Avoid run-on sentences in writing and formal speaking and, if it's not already clear, avoid traveling south of the border without your own big bottle of purified water. Just look at Jill. She was so upset after her travels that she started smoking again.

Party on Prepositional Phrases

I thought I'd go wild in this next section and do something I've never done before! No, I'm not going to dance topless in a cage or swing from a chandelier. But I am going to mix things up a bit and give you the example of a topic before I go into any explanation! Pretty crazy, huh? Maybe by some slim chance, you'll only have to see an example of a prepositional phrase to understand its full meaning and then you can simply skip ahead to the next topic. So let's give this whacky idea a try:

> The disco ball *on the smoky ceiling* is beautiful.

Did you get it? Do you see what's going on here? If so, you can hit the dance floor and celebrate. But for the rest of you who have that dazed look on your faces, I'll go into a bit more detail. The above sentence contains an example of a prepositional phrase. Remember, prepositions are words like *at, by, for, from, in, on, under,* and *nearby.* The purpose of a preposition is to relate a noun or pronoun to another word in a sentence, which helps to expand the meaning of the related word. The noun or pronoun that follows a preposition is called the object of the preposition. Together, the preposition, its object, and any words that modify the object form a prepositional phrase. (For a list of prepositions, see "Puzzling Prepositions" in Chapter 1.)

In the example sentence, *on the smoky ceiling* is a perfect example of a prepositional phrase. The preposition is *on*, its object is *ceiling*, and *the* and *smoky* are modifiers. The preposition relates *disco ball* to the *smoky ceiling*.

Here's another example:

The private party *behind the garage* contains all the cool people.

In this sentence the preposition is *behind*, and its object is *garage*. The preposition relates *party* to *garage*.

A preposition can have two or more objects, as the following example shows:

Tanya left the party *with her raincoat and lovely parting gift.*

In this sentence, the objects of the preposition *with* are *raincoat* and *gift*. The phrase tells *with what* Tanya left the party. *Lovely* and *parting* are adjectives that modify *gift*.

It's not unusual for some prepositional phrases to contain two prepositions that work together, like the example below:

Sherman lifted the heavy keg *out of the box.*

The prepositions in this sentence are *out of* and the object of the preposition is *box*.

Some sentences may contain several prepositional phrases, as this example shows:

Sherman lifted the heavy keg *of beer out of the trunk of his car.*

Three prepositional phrases appear in this sentence: *of beer*, *out of the trunk*, and *of his car*.

Depending on what words they modify, prepositional phrases can function as adjectives or adverbs. A prepositional phrase that modifies a noun or pronoun is an *adjective phrase*. A prepositional phrase that modifies a verb, adjective, or another adverb is, well, you probably guessed it, an *adverb phrase*.

An adjective phrase, like an adjective, answers the questions *what kind? which one?* and *how many?* about a noun or pronoun. An adjective phrase usually follows the noun or pronoun it modifies. Note the examples:

> The hot chick *with blonde hair* walked past me on the way to the food table. (The prepositional phrase modifies *chick*. Which chick? The one with the blonde hair.)
>
> The tall woman *in the low-cut dress* looked familiar. (The prepositional phrase modifies *woman*. Which woman? The one in the low-cut dress.)

Next, let's take a look at an adverb phrase. An adverb phrase, like an adverb, answers the questions *how? when? where? how often?* and *to what extent?* about verbs, adjectives, and other adverbs. Note the examples of prepositional phrases that function as adverbs.

> Steve parties late *at night*. (The prepositional phrase modifies the adverb *late*, and tells when Steve parties.)
>
> Bill and Lorraine left the party *in the morning*. (The prepositional phrase modifies the verb *left*, and tells when they left.)

Just as adverbs can be located at any part of a sentence, depending on its construction, so can adverb phrases. The following examples show different positions of the prepositional phrase.

The lightweights passed out *before midnight*.

Before midnight the lightweights passed out.

Whether they serve as an adjective or an adverb, prepositional phrases allow you to add details to sentences. They give a sentence more pizzazz, just like cage dancers give a party more pizzazz. Just remember the cardinal rule on grammar parties: Never use a prepositional phrase and drive!

How Not to Not, Not Use a Double Negative, AKA How to Not Use One

In the real world, most people would rather be around positive people than negative ones. They'd rather smile than frown. And they'd rather view their martini glass as half full rather than half empty. But in the real world of grammar, it's the negative word that can make a positive statement negative. That might sound confusing, especially if you've just indulged in a martini, so I'll explain in further detail. Here are some of the most common negative words:

neither	none	nowhere
never	no one	barely
no	not (n't)	hardly
nobody	nothing	scarcely

One negative word is sufficient to make an affirmative statement negative. And in keeping with the theme of this classic James Bond beverage, here's an example:

Dixie has a vodka martini. (affirmative)

Dixie does *not* have a vodka martini. (negative)

Not in this sentence is the difference between Dixie having a cocktail and Dixie not needing to find a ride home.

Unlike a double cocktail that just adds to Dixie's drinking problem, a double negative adds to one's grammar problem since double negatives are not a correct way to speak or to write. Here are some examples:

> An apple martini does *not* contain *no* apple juice. (double negative, incorrect)
>
> There will *not* be *no* Happy Hour today because of the blizzard. (double negative, incorrect)
>
> Won't *nobody* open up this jar of olives? (double negative, incorrect)

Double negatives are often used in informal conversations. That's why they slip into ordinary conversation and writing as easily as you slip into your favorite pair of sweats after coming home from a hard day at the office. Sometimes people will use a double negative for emphasis, as if two negative words make a negative statement stronger. But that's not true. Not only are double negatives incorrect usage, the negative words can cancel each other out and may turn the sentence back to an affirmative. Consider this example:

> We don't have *no* more vermouth.

Not having *no* vermouth implies that we actually do have vermouth, so the intent of the sentence is magically reversed. Speaking in double negatives is understandable after having a few martinis but is nonetheless confusing to both listeners and readers.

Luckily, unlike other problems in life, like earthquakes, crime, and hard-to-open bags of potato chips, this problem

> **❝** We were at a pie shop and I asked for a slice of apple. The waitress answered in a double negative that they didn't have no apple. Just to give her a hard time I said, 'great, I'd love a slice.' She kept trying to tell me they didn't have any and I kept trying to be funny. I ended up ordering strawberry pie instead but was afraid to eat it since I figured there was a good chance she spit in it just to get even. **❞**
>
> —Carl

is solved very easily. Simply drop one of the negative words, or replace a negative word with an acceptable affirmative word. Note the examples:

> We don't have vermouth today.
> We have *no* vermouth today.
> We don't have *any* vermouth today.

Before you go off and use your knowledge of double negatives for good and not evil, remember that *hardly*, *scarcely*, and *barely* are also negative words. But because they don't contain the word *no*, their true nature can easily be overlooked. For instance:

> Dixie is a cheap date and hardly never has more than one drink. (double negative)
> Dixie is a cheap date and hardly ever has more than one drink. (correct)
> Men can't barely help noticing. (double negative)
> Men can barely help noticing. (correct)

As if hardly, scarcely, and barely aren't tricky enough, you must also pay close attention to *can't help but*, *haven't but*, and *haven't only*, each of which results in a double negative. Note the example:

> Single guys can't help but ask Dixie out. (double negative)
>
> Single guys can't help asking Dixie out. (correct)

So remember, always avoid double negatives in conversation and writing since they're *never* considered to be examples of good grammar. And more importantly, always keep vermouth handy if you're fond of this classic cocktail.

grammatical hot topics: global warming in english form

When you're driving down the road, there are many signs to follow that help guide you along your way. They instruct you to stop, to yield, to merge, and to get to a nearby McDonald's. When you speak, you do the same thing. As you talk, you arrange words into sentences and phrases by pauses and inflections and insert verbal signs on how the listener should follow them. Longer pauses indicate the end of a sentence; shorter pauses indicate the end of a clause or a phrase. Subtle inflections, the rising or falling of your voice, may indicate emphasis, emotion, or tone. Such pauses and inflections show punctuation. They cue listeners and help them find meaning in your spoken words.

Problematic Punctuation

In written English, these signs, or punctuation marks, are crucial. Sure, they won't tell you where you can find the closest Big Mac, but they are nonetheless important.

Punctuation marks substitute for the pauses and inflections and help to make the writer's expression clear.

So, while you need not worry about punctuation when speaking (unless you're one of those people who holds up two fingers on each hand when you're quoting someone), you absolutely need to know punctuation when writing. If Bill sent a letter that was riddled with punctuation errors to a prospective employer, he'd no doubt ruin his chance of getting the job . . . unless, of course, he's applying for a job flipping burgers.

English punctuation marks are divided into several types. The most common ones include:

- End marks (periods, question marks, and exclamation points)
- Commas
- Colons
- Semicolons
- Quotation marks
- Italics (underlining)
- Apostrophes
- Hyphens
- Parentheses
- Dashes

Although you're no doubt familiar with each one to some degree, let's take this time to examine them all in full detail. What else do we have to do, anyway?

End Marks

End marks consist of periods, question marks, and exclamation points. They have several uses so let's go through them one by one.

Use a period:
- To end a declarative sentence (statement).
  Bill got that job at McDonalds.

- To end an imperative sentence (command).
  Be at work at nine sharp.

- With initials.
  J. K. Rowling

- At the end of an abbreviation.
  Mr.
  A.M.
  St.

- With money and measurements.
  $29.95
  7.5 meters

- Don't use periods with acronyms or all uppercase abbreviations.
  ASAP
  BLT

- When using abbreviations in writing, leave only one space after the period.

special note regarding end marks: When directly quoting a sentence, end marks go inside quotation marks.

Use a question mark:
- To end an interrogative sentence (question), or a sentence that requests confirmation.

    Did you want fries with that?

Use an exclamation point:
- To end a sentence showing strong emotion.

    Yuk! There's a hair in my McFlurrie!

- To end a sentence showing strong emphasis, sarcasm, or astonishment.

    Oh no!
    Bill said, "Oh oh, I can't find my hair net!"

However, if the quotation is a sentence set within a statement or question, the end mark is placed outside the quotation marks.

Are you familiar with the expression, "You're fired"?

Commas

Speaking of McDonald's, you could say that the comma is the McDonald's of punctuation. It's popular and used by millions of people each and every day. Because commas have so many uses, mastering the comma can be a true challenge. Learning the following guidelines will help you to use commas correctly.

Use commas:

- To separate words, phrases, and clauses in a series.

  lions, tigers, and bears (oh my!)

  On their first date, he told her about his job, his family, his experience in rehab, and his stint in prison.

- Before a coordinating conjunction (*and, but, or, nor, for,* or *yet*) that separates two independent clauses.

  Do you want to watch the repeat of *I Love Lucy* for the eighth time, or do you want to watch the rerun of *Seinfeld* for the ninth?

- To set off an introductory clause or phrase.

  After Tom Cruise jumped on Oprah's couch, demand for interviews with the actor skyrocketed. (introductory dependent clause)

  We ate at a restaurant *that won several awards for its seafood specialties.*

  Soon after that incident, Tom was thought to be a lovesick freak.

  On Monday his wife had PMS.

- To set off introductory words such as *yes, no, oh, well, also, still, now,* and *why* in a sentence. Examples:

  Yes, dear, I'll be at home by six.

  No, I don't want to pick up the dry cleaning on my way home.

- To set off nonessential clauses or phrases in a sentence. Nonessential material is information that can be left out of a sentence without changing the meaning of the sentence. These are also called nonrestrictive elements.

CAUTION

Special note regarding commas and clauses: While a comma is necessary after an introductory clause, do not use a comma to set off an essential clause that appears within the sentence.

The beginning of the football season, *which is the worst time of year for many wives,* will start next week.

> **CAUTION !**
>
> **special note:** After an introductory clause or phrase, the comma separates the introductory material from the subject of the sentence. This makes it easier for the reader to subconsciously identify the subject, which in turn makes it easier to understand the meaning of the sentence. In cases where introductory material is short and the subject is clear, you don't need the comma.

Note that *which is the worst time of year for many wives* is not essential to the sentence. As such, it needs to be separated from the rest of the sentence by commas.

The Oompa Loompas' boss, *Willie Wonka,* is easy to work for.

To set off words used in direct address such as:

Mr. Wonka, Violet ate some gum and turned into a blueberry.

It's a good idea, *Augustus,* not to stand too close to the chocolate river.

A comma is also used to set off parenthetical expressions. Parenthetical expressions are words added to a sentence for emphasis or clarity. Common parenthetical expressions include:

after all	I believe (assume, hope, etc.)
as a matter of fact	in addition
by the way	in fact
consequently	in my opinion
for example	nevertheless

for instance	of course
furthermore	on the other hand
however	therefore

Since I've started this Wonka thing, I'll run with it awhile longer. Here are some examples of parenthetical expressions:

Of course, your whole family can live at the factory.

As a matter of fact, I don't like old people, but your grandparents can come too.

> **CAUTION**
>
> **special note:** *An appositive is a word or phrase that follows a noun or pronoun and identifies, explains, or provides additional information about the noun or pronoun. Appositives must be set off with commas.*

- To separate modifiers of equal importance.

  The *calm, tranquil* river of chocolate didn't look as treacherous as it turned out to be.

- To separate items in dates.

  Wednesday, the 15th of July, 2007

- To separate elements in place names and addresses.

  Hershey, Pennsylvania

  123 Sesame Street, New York, NY 12345

- To set off direct quotations in a sentence, and to set off speaker tags such as *said Charlie.*

"I can't wait to go in the glass elevator," said Charlie.

"I hope we build up enough speed to get through the roof," said Mr. Wonka, "but I doubt it."

- To set off degrees or titles following a person's name.

  Mr. Jim James, Jr. is vice president of marketing.

- After the opening of a friendly letter and after the closing of all letters.

  Dear Grandpa Joe,

  Yours truly,

- In numbers of more than three digits.

  1,034

  106,485

Colons

A colon is not just a word to snicker at in junior high school health class. It's also an important punctuation mark that means "note what follows." Although colons are certainly not used with the frequency of commas, they're necessary for specific instances.

Use a colon:
- Before a list but not after a verb or preposition.

  Martha Stewart packed the following items for the picnic: wilted green salad, fennel tuna sandwiches, orzo rice with spring peas, and a peach tart. (correct)

  Martha Stewart packed: corn dogs, fried bologna sandwiches, potato salad with extra mayo, and Moon Pies for the picnic. (incorrect because the colon follows the verb *packed*, and because Martha would never be seen making such white-trash food)

- Between independent clauses when the second clause explains the first.

  Being in Camp Cupcake has caused a big change: she is now seen as a nice person.

- To introduce a quotation, particularly a long and formal statement.

  Martha announced to her staff: "This month's magazine will have several articles. One will delve into the mystery of spot removal. Another will explore the history of the San Marzano tomato, the best tomato for sauce. And the last one will be about how to crochet a decorative poncho out of compost."

- In time.

  2:30 P.M.

- Between volume and page of a magazine, chapter and verse of the Bible, and similar designations.

  29:16 (volume 29, page 16)

  Genesis 1:28

- In certain titles.

  Part I:
  A Nation Awakes

  Chapter 22:
  Awareness

- In ratios.

  4:1

  3:4

- In the salutation (greeting) of a business letter.

  Dear Ms. Wilson:

To Whom It May Concern:

- In letter and memo headings.
  To:
  From:
  Subject:

Semicolons

I find that the semicolon is like one of those intimidating food processors you get as a wedding gift. Since you're never quite sure how to use it, you end up never using it and cutting everything by hand anyway (or you do use it and end up cutting your hand!). But once understood, a semicolon is really quite simple (as is the food processor, but it does take a bit of getting used to). The main purpose of a semicolon is to indicate a pause. In a way, it functions much like end marks and commas, but the pause indicated by a semicolon isn't quite as long as an end mark and not as brief as the pause of a comma. Like all punctuation, however, the semicolon has distinct uses in a sentence.

Use a semicolon:
- To separate independent clauses not linked by a coordinating conjunction.

  Simon Cowell believes in judging the *American Idol* contestants harshly; Paula Abdul believes in being nice to everyone.

- To separate independent clauses connected by a conjunctive adverb such as *however*, *therefore*, *nevertheless*, *furthermore*, and *consequently*.

Simon and Paula flirt constantly; *however*, the two swear that they are not a couple.

- In a series with internal punctuation. In a complex series, it may be hard for readers to know if commas are a part of items or are separating the items. In such cases, semicolons can be used to separate the items.

  Simon is hated around the country but especially in Atlanta, one of his favorite cities; Houston, where he loves the food; and Phoenix, where he loves the climate.

- Between independent clauses if commas are in one or both of the clauses.

  Viewers love *American Idol*, a unique show that gives a nobody a chance to become a star; and best of all, that new star gets the opportunity to host a TV Christmas special.

Quotation Marks

The main use of quotation marks is to indicate a person's exact words. But they can serve a dual purpose because they can also be used for emphasis or to enclose the names of various short works.

Use quotation marks:
- To enclose a person's exact words, called a *direct quotation*. Don't use quotation marks to enclose an indirect quotation, because that's not a person's exact words.

  "I am not a crook," said Nixon. (direct quotation)
  Nixon said that he is not a crook. (indirect quotation)

In the second example, someone else is saying what they heard Nixon say, but he's not saying Nixon's exact words. Use of the word *that* indicates an indirect quotation.

"I'd like to believe him," said the vice president, "but there's so much evidence to the contrary."

Note the comma before *said* and that *but* is lowercase. If the author wanted a slightly longer pause, she would write it as follows.

"I'd like to believe him," the vice president said. "But there's so much evidence to the contrary."

- To enclose titles of articles, short stories, poems, songs, and chapters of books.

  "Danke Shoen" was playing on the radio when we first kissed.

  I remember blushing a lot when I was a kid and read chapter 5, "Aphrodisiacs," in my parent's copy of *Everything You Always Wanted to Know about Sex*.

- For emphasis with special words or descriptions.

  E-mail, or "electronic mail," is the best way to advertise for penile enhancements.

  I couldn't believe my conservative granny was once a "flower child."

  "I have a hot date this weekend," said Lisa, "so I have to lose twenty pounds in the next three days."

Question marks and exclamation points are placed inside quotation marks if they're a part of the direct quotation. If they're not a part of the direct quotation, they're placed outside.

Special note: *If a quotation is interrupted by tag words, such as he said or she said, each part of the quotation must be enclosed in quotation marks.*

"Will he take you to dinner?" asked Sheri.

Didn't you say, "He will take Sheri to dinner"?

Semicolons are always placed outside quotation marks.

Walking into the lobby was Lisa's "hot date"; but, in my opinion, he only proved that beauty is in the eye of the beholder.

For showing a quotation within a quotation, single quotation marks are used.

"Lisa said, 'I'm going to become a lesbian,'" said Sheri.

Special note for using quotation marks: *Periods and commas are always placed inside quotation marks.*

Italics

Italics are used to indicate creative works that are packaged individually and sold to the public, names of some vehicles, foreign words and phrases, and words requiring emphasis. *Italics also indicate that you have to bend your head to the right a little in order to read words because italics are letters that lean to the right in printed material, just like this sentence, and I bet your head is tilted a little bit to the right while you're reading it.*

In instances where *italic* type cannot be used, <u>underlining</u> may be used to indicate italics.

Use italics for:

- Books:
  The Da Vinci Code

- Magazines
  Star magazine

- Newspapers
  The New York Times

- E-zines
  Salon

- Long poems
  Paradise Lost

- Movies
  Dumb and Dumber

- TV Programs
  Saturday Night Live

- Plays
  The Vagina Monologues

- Paintings
  The Mona Lisa

- Sculptures
  David

- Operas
  The Barber of Seville

- Computer games: *Doom*
- Online works: *Encarta*
- Ships: USS *Constitution*
- Spacecraft: *Starship Enterprise*
- Trains: *Orient Express*
- Planes: *Concorde*
- Foreign words and phrases unless they have become highly Anglicized and commonly recognized

Columbo's modus operandi was odd and puzzling, but he always got his perp.

- Referring to words as words

  People often misuse the words *lay* and *lie*.

- Emphasis

  Now *that's* Italian!

Apostrophes

Apostrophes are good for many things. They're a good way to show possession, or ownership, for nouns and indefinite pronouns; they can indicate omitted letters for contractions; and they're good for indicating the plural of letters, symbols, and numbers. They are not good, however, for getting out of speeding tickets, so know their limitations.

Use an apostrophe:

- To indicate the possessive case of singular nouns. With most singular nouns, the possessive case is formed by adding an apostrophe and *s*.

  Trump's comb-over
  Cindy Crawford's mole

Keep in mind that when a singular noun of more than one syllable ends in an *s*-sound, the apostrophe may be added without adding the *s*. For example, the witness' subpoena, Mr. Rogers' Neighborhood.

- To indicate the possessive case of plural nouns. With plural nouns that end in *s*, the possessive case is formed by only adding an apostrophe. For plural nouns that don't end in *s*, the possessive case is formed by adding an apostrophe and an *s*.

the three puppies' bed

the children's bikes

Keep in mind that when dealing with compound nouns and words that share joint possession, only the last word takes the possessive form.

brother-in-law's business

Bill and Wanda's ranch

In cases where two or more nouns possess something as individuals, each takes the possessive form.

Clinton's and Bush's foreign policy programs [meaning Clinton's foreign policy program and Bush's foreign policy program; not the combined programs of both presidents]

Ted's and Josh's birthdays are in November [meaning Ted's birthday and Josh's birthday are both in November]

- To indicate the possessive case of indefinite pronouns (examples being *one, anyone, everyone, someone, everybody, nobody*, and *no one*). The possessive case is formed the same way as nouns.

  Someone's dentures are on the table.

  Are these *anyone's* dentures?

- To indicate the plural of letters, numbers, symbols, and words referred to as words.

  Mississippi has four S's, four I's, and two P's.

  Sue had all A's and +'s on her report card.

  Many people are blaming *HMOs* for all that is bad in the world.

> **❝** When I got married I took my husband's last name of Gross. I have no idea how to make it possessive. Is it Grosses? Gross's? I've never been able to get anything engraved because I'm too embarrassed to admit to the salesperson that I don't know how to spell my last name. **❞**
>
> —Amy

ATMs are a great place to hang out if you want to get mugged.

- To indicate possessive adjectives that show time and amount required.

  a *week's* vacation

  five hundred *dollars'* worth of clothes

- To indicate omitted letters in contractions.

  I am/I'm

  we are/we're

  it is/it's (not to be confused with *its*)

  you are/you're (not to be confused with *your*)

  does not/doesn't

  cannot/can't

  will not/won't

  they are/they're (not to be confused with *there* or *their*)

  have not/haven't

  must not/mustn't

  should not/shouldn't

  the 1960s/the '60s

Special note: *For some plurals—for example, numbers referring to decades and initializations—apostrophes are not used.*

Avoiding Controversy with Contractions

While we're discussing apostrophes and involvement in contractions, let me give you a few tips on how to use them correctly. Don't worry—there are no polysyllabic terms to learn, no confusing rules to decipher, and no stupid jokes about Hollywood gossip or TV trivia. Instead, this is a section that's meant to give you a breather in between your mental workouts. So I'll go easy on you here as we talk about contractions.

What is a contraction anyway? A *contraction* is a shortened form of a word, or words, which is then used as a single word. An apostrophe is used to indicate an omitted letter, or letters. The apostrophe in a contraction is always placed precisely at the spot where the letters were omitted.

Some of the most commonly used contractions include:

aren't = are not	should've = should have
can't = cannot	there's = there is
couldn't = could not	they'd = they had
doesn't = does not	they've = they have
don't = do not	we're = we are
hadn't = had not	we've = we have
hasn't = has not	where's = where is
haven't = have not	who's = who is
here's = here is	won't = will not
I'm = I am	would've = would have

isn't = is not	you'd = you had
it's = it is	you're = you are
mustn't = must not	you've = you have

See? Not too stressful so far. You just relax and stretch while I continue. The use of contractions tends to give speaking and writing an informal tone. Although contractions pepper conversational speaking and writing, they should be avoided in formal writing because of their casual, laissez-faire informality.

One problem of contractions is when there's a lack of agreement between subjects and verbs. Here are some examples of common contractions used in a faulty way.

> He don't have any relaxing music.
>
> Here's your towels for your massage.

In most cases, substituting the words that make up the contraction in the sentence will help you to determine the correct form. Here are the corrected examples:

> He *don't* have any relaxing music. (incorrect)
>
> He *do not* have any relaxing music. (incorrect)
>
> He *doesn't* (*does not*) have any relaxing music. (correct)

In this example, *does* is the correct form of the verb, because it agrees with the singular subjective case pronoun *he*.

> *Here's* your towels for your massage. (incorrect)
>
> *Here is* your towels for your massage. (incorrect)
>
> *Here are* your towels for your massage. (correct)

In the previous example, *Here are* is necessary, because *towels* is the subject of the sentence and requires the plural form of the verb, *are*. In fact, it's even correct to say *Here're your towels for your massage*, although it sounds a bit awkward. But you may be in too much of a relaxed state to even notice. Here's another common example of the incorrect usage of contractions:

I ain't going to work today.

The word *ain't* is used as a contraction for *am not, is not, are not, has not,* and *have not*. Although the word *ain't* is a common word on the WB network, it isn't considered to be a part of Standard English and isn't a part of formal speech. Therefore, it's generally wise to avoid using *ain't* in both speaking and writing, unless you write for shows on the WB network.

Another problem with many contractions is confusing them with another word:

Were leaving for the movies at eight.

In this sentence, the apostrophe for *we're* was omitted. This is a common oversight in writing that results in a glaring mistake. Concentration and careful proofreading can catch these kinds of errors, except of course after a relaxing smoothie and a massage.

The final problem writers can encounter when using contractions focuses on confusing certain possessive pronouns with contractions, like the ones in the following examples:

it's (it is) and *its*
you're (you are) and *your*
they're (they are) and *their* (or *there*)
who's (who is) and *whose*

I know these always mess me up. I, like most people, think that contractions are so simple that I skip right over them, focusing more on the larger grammatical picture. But knowing that these fundamental issues occur can lessen occurrence. I hope that you've enjoyed this mentally relaxing section on contractions, because it's time to get your butt in gear and back on the Grammartron once again!

Hyphens

Hyphens have two main purposes in a sentence—to punctuate certain compound words and to divide words at the end of a line.

Use a hyphen:

- To hyphenate certain compound words. Compound words are words that are formed by joining two or more words. They may be closed (with no spaces between them), open (with a space between them), or hyphenated.

  daydream (closed)

  eye shadow (open)

  all-time, up-to-date, mother-in-law (hyphenated)

- To write a compound adjective when it precedes the noun or pronoun it modifies—but not after.

  the well-known author (not *the author was well-known*)

  a little-known law (not *the law is little-known*)

  the widely renowned scientist

- With the prefixes ex-, self-, and all-, and the termination -elect.

  ex-lover

self-confidence

president-elect

- Between any prefix and a proper noun or adjective.

mid-January

pre-Etruscan culture

- To avoid awkward vowel or triple consonants, both of which can make confusing-looking words.

semi-invalid, not semiinvalid

pre-emergent, not preemergent

bell-like and not belllike

- To divide a word at the end of a line. This use is becoming somewhat obsolete, however, as word processing software generally wraps words around to the next line. If you do divide words, be sure to divide them only between syllables and never divide words so that only one letter ends or begins a line. For further help, consult a dictionary.

Tori Spelling is tangible proof that ne-

potism doesn't get you as far in life as one would hope. (incorrect)

Tori Spelling is tangible proof that nep-

otism doesn't get you as far in life as one would hope. (correct)

- To write compound numbers from twenty-one to ninety-nine.

one hundred eighty-six

Special note: To ensure you're using compound words correctly, consult a dictionary. Spell checkers in word processing programs may or may not tag hyphenated words.

- To write fractions used as adjectives.

    one-half pound

    three-fourths cup

Parentheses

Parentheses house the words of the sentence that aren't as important as the other ones and therefore aren't a part of the popular "in" group. The information enclosed by parentheses may be a number, a single word, or a brief sentence.

Special note: *Don't use a hyphen when one of the modifiers is an adverb (remember, those usually end in –ly).*

Examples:

Many men consider Marilyn Monroe (1926–1962) to be one of America's most beautiful women.

The human heart (see figure 3) is about the size of the average individual's fist.

Winona Ryder's shopping spree (if that's what you want to call it!) was certainly newsworthy.

Dashes

Dashes are used primarily to indicate a break in thought or to signal a coming explanation. They should be used sparingly. If you know about cooking, you can think of them as the powerful herb cilantro. Overuse of dashes makes writing seem choppy, and overuse of cilantro makes food taste just plain yucky.

Use dashes:
- To indicate a break in thought.

  Most drag queens—even the new ones—have perfected the mannerisms of Barbra Streisand.

  Liza Minnelli—who used to be the favorite of the bunch—now comes in a distant second.

- To signal a coming explanation that would otherwise be introduced by words such as *that is* or *in other words*.

  The reason that Liza lost her great appeal was because of that horrible incident—when she gave that disgusting wedding day kiss to new hubby, David Gest.

- To set off an internal list of items.

  Liza had many witnesses of this incident—Michael Jackson, Barbara Walters, Elizabeth Taylor—all of whom were physically sickened.

Somewhat Uncommon Punctuation Marks

Now that we've discussed some of the most popular forms of punctuation, let's go over the ones that tend to be lesser known and hang out with the chess and audio/visual clubs. Even though these lesser known forms of punctuation are not as popular, you should still be aware of these useful punctuation marks.

Brackets

Brackets are used primarily to insert clarification into quotations or to insert information into material that's already enclosed in parentheses.

Use brackets:
- To insert clarifying material into a direct quotation.

Special notes: *The use of commas and dashes is often interchangeable with the use of parentheses. This is especially true when setting off minor words or phrases. Also, punctuation marks can be within parentheses when they belong with the parenthetical material. Punctuation that belongs to the sentence as a whole, however, shouldn't be placed within parentheses.*

> "The punk rock group Death by Maggots [formerly known as Death by Aphids] will be performing at the Grove Stadium this Tuesday."

Without clarification, readers might not realize that this is the same group. Note that the material in the brackets has been inserted by an editor and not the speaker or author of the quotation. If the material was included by the author, parentheses should be used.

With the word *sic*, which means *so* or *thus* and is used to indicate an error in grammar, usage, or spelling in a quotation. Here again, the clarification is inserted by an editor and not the speaker or author of the quotation.

> In criticizing the group's prices for the upcoming concert, one irate fan wrote: "I believe the high ticket prices are a way to keep guys like I [*sic*] who don't have more than a fifth-grade education from sitting next to rich, smart people."

Imagine this being a newspaper article in which the reporter quoted the fan's letter. The fan should have written "me" instead of "I," and the reporter doesn't want people to think that he (the reporter) is responsible for the mistake. He also doesn't want his boss to think that he (the reporter) only has a fifth-grade education as well.

- To indicate emphasis with a quotation, added by an editor and not the speaker or author of the words.

"Many years ago, groups like Death by Maggots were seen as normal and acceptable forms of music. Now, they're seen as nothing but *freaks of nature*"[emphasis added].

- For parenthetical information within parentheses.

    "Mt. Everest, the highest mountain in the world (8,848 m [29,028 ft]), is no longer the most inaccessible."

Ellipses

An ellipsis is a fancy-schmancy name for a series of three periods. It indicates a gap in a quotation or a pause in a sentence. An ellipsis is pretty straightforward. The only things you have to remember about it is that if a sentence ends in an ellipsis, you need to use four dots. And, to pluralize the word, you have to end it in *es* (ellipses).

Use an ellipsis:
- To indicate a deletion of material from a quotation.

    "When the Beatles started out years back, John Lennon, Paul McCartney, George Harrison, and Ringo Starr . . . performed at the local pubs." The material, *who replaced original drummer Pete Best*, is left out of the sentence (not to mention that Pete Best is left out of a lifetime of fame and fortune). The omission is indicated by the ellipsis.

- To indicate a pause in a sentence, most often for dramatic emphasis.

    Pete Best continued with a musical career and was known around the world . . . as the guy who missed out on being a Beatle.

- To indicate the trailing off of a thought.

    They always meant to look up how to spell "beetle" in the dictionary, but sometimes, the best laid plans. . . .

The Slash

A slash is a way to show alternatives such as he/she, him/her, owner/operator, or wife/mother/executive. Although slashes have their uses, in most cases they can easily be replaced with a comma or the word *or*.

Chapter 4

the A-B-C's of H-E-L-L

Up until this point, I've tried to add a touch of humor to the otherwise humorless subject of grammar. But as hard as I tried, I couldn't find a hook to make the subject of capitals anything more than a dry and straightforward part of the English language. So let's just get this topic over with as quickly as possible, sort of like pulling off a Band-Aid, jumping into a cold pool, or having sex with your husband when you're really not in the mood. Here are the rules of capitals.

Putting the "Caps" on Capitalization

Capital letters (also called uppercase letters) focus on marking the beginning of sentences, proper nouns—specific people, places, things, or ideas—and abbreviations. Here are plenty of pointers.

Always capitalize:

- The pronoun *I*.
- The first word in any sentence.
- The first word of a complete sentence that's used in a direct quote.

  Samantha asked, "Where exactly is Funkytown?"

- The names of persons or pets.

  George Washington, Cher, Fluffy

Special notes: *When a sentence follows a colon or a dash, capitalization of the first word is optional. Also, sentence fragments that are placed inside of parentheses in a sentence (like what I'm doing right now) are not capitalized. If a separate sentence is placed in parentheses, the first word of the sentence within the parentheses should be capitalized. (See, here's a separate sentence and it's capitalized.) The first word of a fragment used as a question or for emphasis should always be capitalized. No exceptions to this rule.*

- Initials.

  Harry S Truman, A. A. Milne, Alfred E. Neuman

- The names of continents, countries, states, cities, counties, towns, and similar entities.

  Asia

  United States of America

  Japan

  New Jersey

  London

  Harper County

- Geographical names.
  the Pacific Ocean
  the South Hudson Valley
  the Rocky Mountains
  the Nile River
  Timbuktu
  the Sahara Desert
  the Arctic

- Particular places, things, and ideas.
  Grand Central Station, the White House, Sandy's Strip Joint
  the Golden Gate Bridge, Red Light District
  Equal Rights

Special note: *Words like of and the, unless they are part of or start the name, are generally not capitalized.*

- Titles of people when they precede a name and the abbreviations *Sr.* and *Jr.* after a name.
  Captain John Smith, Dr. Samantha Martin, Professor O'Hara
  Harry Connick, Jr.

- The names of the months, days, and holidays.
  January
  Sunday
  Thanksgiving, Bring Your Child to Work Day

Special note: *Compass directions (north, northeast, northeasterly, etc.) are capitalized only when they're a part of a name, like South Africa, or when they're used for a specific region, like the Northeast.*

- The names of historical events, periods (but not the four seasons), and documents.

  the Dark Ages, the Renaissance, World War II

- The names of government bodies, organizations, companies, and institutions.

  the United Nations (UN), The Betty Ford Clinic, Girl Scouts

- The names of specific objects, products, and vehicles.

  the Orion Nebula, Jeep Liberty, *Queen Elizabeth 2*, Pictionary

Special note: *Capitalize brand names but not the name of the product, for example, Turkey Hill ice cream. Also, some companies use intercaps for certain products, such as WordPerfect or Microsoft PowerPoint. In addition, some companies use all caps in their abbreviated names, such as AOL. In these cases, be sure to follow the company's usage.*

- Religions, religious holidays or celebrations, and holy books.

  Catholicism, Islam, Judaism

  Christmas, Ramadan, Passover

  Holy Communion, the Koran, the Bible

- Words referring to the Deity, Christ, and Mary.

  God the Father, Jehovah, the Virgin Mary, the Messiah

- Nationalities, languages, and races.

  Irish, English, Chinese, Swahili

- Proper adjectives.

  Mexican food, Russian history, Islamic nations

- Names of awards, prizes, and medals.

  the Nobel Prize, a Golden Globe, the Purple Heart

Special notes: *Personal pronouns referring to the Deity are usually capitalized (He, His, and Him). Relative pronouns (who, whom, and whose) are usually not capitalized. Don't capitalize the word god when referring to any of the gods of the pre-Christian world, for example, the gods and goddesses of Ancient Greece. However, you should capitalize their individual names (Zeus, Apollo, Hera, etc.).*

- The first, last, and all important words in titles.
  Gone with the Wind, "The Raven," *Grammar Sucks*

- Special events.
  the World Series, the Boston Marathon, One-Day Sale

- All letters of acronyms and most abbreviations.
  NASA, CPA, P.O. Box, IUD, STD

- All of the words of the greeting of a letter, but only the first word of the closing of a letter.
  Dear Aunt Grace, Dear Mr. Herman, Forget you ever knew me,

- Parts of a compound word as if each stands alone.
  anti-American feelings, Spanish-American War

There! It's over! The Band-Aid is off, you've jumped into the pool, and your husband's rolled over and is already asleep! You made it through this dry section on capitals and are ready to move onto this next sensational subject.

Can You Use Slang and Still Have "Bad" Grammar?

I've heard that English is one of the hardest languages to learn. That's difficult to imagine since I've seen two-year-olds speak near fluent English, and they can barely find their thumb. One reason our language is hard to learn is that it's riddled with so much slang that keeping up with this ever-increasing sublanguage is nearly impossible (yes, I'm sure that other languages contain slang as well, but since the only foreign phrase I know is Haagen Dazs, we'll stick to English for now).

Along with standard English, there are many sub-versions of English, and slang is one of the most common ones. Slang refers to words and expressions used primarily by a subgroup or subculture. Teenagers are a perfect example. This rebellious group of human beings uses colorful words to express a specific meaning, and they have throughout time. What they once called "nifty" then became "rad" and is now called "phat."

Many slang words are not grammatically correct. But there are exceptions. Some slang words like cool (as in excellent) and fox (as in a desirable woman) have been accepted into the English language and are even recognized by most dictionaries, which often make note of the entered word and definition as "slang." This does not mean, however, that it's a good idea to use slang in your speaking and writing. For one thing, if you're over thirty, using words like "gnarly" can reveal your true age as accurately as cutting you in half and counting your rings. For another, the slang you use may not be understood by those people who are "outside" of your group. For instance, if some high school kid asked me for "cheddar," I'd surely hand him a wedge of sharp cheese instead of the cold hard cash that he was asking me for.

Although there are many instances where using slang is appropriate, like when you're among your peers or at a VH1 awards show, there are still more places where it would be perceived as inappropriate. Like in places of worship, places of business, and any place that your strict mother hangs out.

"One of the worst parts about getting old is that you don't know the hip language anymore. Last week when my teenage son had some friends over, I excused myself saying that I had to go send a fax. They all cracked up like it was the funniest thing they ever heard. My son later informed me that send a fax is slang for defecate. Kids these days.**"**

—Alan

Even though using slang is fine when you're around people who understand it, it's best to avoid using it at all when speaking or writing to someone that you're trying to impress. For if you tell someone that they're looking "bad" when you mean that they're looking good, it will certainly make you look pretty "bad."

What's Grammatically Legal?

In the judicial system, things are pretty much straightforward. If you use a gun, you go to prison. If you embezzle funds, you go to prison. And if you commit murder, you go to prison . . . except of course if you're a celebrity who can afford a high-powered attorney who can bend the law in your favor as easily as he can bend a pipe cleaner.

But things are not so clear-cut when it comes to the English language. With every rule, there are many exceptions to that rule. For instance, have you ever wondered why the plural of *goose* is *geese* but the plural of *moose* isn't *meece*? Or why we have one *deer* and two *deer*, but not two *deers*? Or why a comma is placed inside quotation marks, but a semicolon never is? Or why you always seem to get pudding on your new blouse but never on your old sweatpants? The exceptions can go on and on with little logic, riddling the rules of English grammar with loopholes big enough to drive a Hummer through.

The reason that there are so many exceptions to so many rules is that the English language is like the hole in the ozone layer: It's constantly growing and expanding. Along with absorbing words from Roman Latin (which a few hundred years earlier had absorbed words from ancient Greek), English is bursting with words from at least fifty major languages. It's been estimated that a thousand years ago English consisted of only about 40,000 words. Today, a fair-sized English dictionary contains well over a half million. A good many of these words were added to the language as England grew in prominence and power. As the Brits traveled the oceans and continents in hopes of setting up colonies, they took English with them and absorbed thousands of new words along the way. As words from other languages were melted in, and more words were invented to describe the new things they saw like different kinds of plants and topless Tahitian women, they didn't always fit in with old Anglo-Saxon, which is the language from which modern English arose. Because of its extensive vocabulary and the vast areas in which English was spoken, dialects and colloquialisms naturally occurred. The spoken language didn't always follow the so-called rules, so people became more lax in the interpretation of grammar.

Poets are the most deviant "grammar breakers" of all, using poetic license as an excuse to throw caution to the wind. Some poems follow a specific form with rhythm and rhyme patterns; others are free of any form. Some lines in a poem begin with a capital letter while others don't. Some poems follow the rules of punctuation while others have no punctuation at all. And some poems make sense while others sound like a bunch of horse pituki that you're expected to love no matter how stupid you think it really is. As you can see, standards are ignored in the search for creative expression.

This brings us back to the question of "What's grammatically legal?" What will get you a slap on the wrist and what will send you up the grammar river? Like the Supreme Court's five-to-four decision, there's nothing definitive; there are no rules for breaking the rules, but here are some guidelines:

- Speak or write in a manner and style that will be understood by your audience. For example, speaking to the department heads of a major company requires a stricter adherence to grammatical rules than does a drunken conversation during poker night with the guys.
- If you do break any of the rules of grammar, make sure that you have a good reason for doing so and that listeners or readers will find your rule-breaking insightful, and not cause for teasing you unmercifully for years to come.

There's an old saying: "Rules are made to be broken." The rebel in you might be cheered by such a statement, but before you go off on a grammar-breaking binge, be sure you understand what you're doing. You don't want to spend years in Grammar Prison for absentmindedly breaking a rule. For if you're not careful, you could spend decades being incarcerated alongside other felons who committed grammar faux pas like dangled participles and sentences ended with a preposition.

Part 2

intermediate stuff: or, grammar basics you should know if you're going after that promotion

Good-bye part 1, hello part 2. The mere fact that you've gotten this far proves to me that you're a disciplined student who pays close attention to detail. Either that or you like to skip around a lot when you read. Now that we're done with the fundamentals of grammar, let's take things to a higher level . . . a level filled with more frustrating grammar rules! This second section of the book is designed to take what you've just learned, mix the information up with a few rules, and start applying it in a sentence. After reading these more complicated and higher concepts of grammar, you'll have a far superior grasp of the subtleties of our language. You'll be able to write a more professional-sounding speech. You'll be able to impress a potential employer with your grasp of the English language. And best of all, you'll be able to talk

yourself out of a moving violation whenever a police offi-
cer pulls you over. Well, not really. If grammar really did
that, then every sixteen-year-old would talk like Professor
Higgins from *My Fair Lady*. But it can really give you the
power to do the other things. Keep in mind that as you read
this second section of the book, you may recognize items
that we've mentioned in the first section. I know your first
response will be to say that there's no way in H-E-double
toothpicks that you're going to reread any grammar stuff . . .
that would just be too cruel! But relax. Even though there
may be a concept or two that has been explained previously,
it is only used as a sounding board to launch you into an
even more complicated aspect of grammar!

Chapter 5

it's all in the details

Just as every man has a dream and every Twinkie has its creamy center, every sentence must also have its two essential parts: the subject and the predicate. (See, I told you I'd get to them here.) If either part is missing, you end up having only a fragment of a sentence, which is not a sentence at all. Although this scenario is bad, it's not nearly as catastrophic as if the Twinkie was missing its creamy center, since then all you'd have is a boring chunk of yellow cake. It seems that if you're going to speak and write with correct sentences, you're going to need to understand just how subjects and predicates work. And one key ingredient in this puzzle is making sure that subjects, and the verbs that make up the predicate, agree in number.

On the Subject of Subjects and Predicates
Back in your early days of school when you were learning important lessons in life like sharing, following rules, and that paste makes a scrumptious midday treat, your teacher no doubt explained to you that the subject of a sentence is

the doer of the action and the predicate is the action. Now that you're an adult, we can expand that simple theory a bit. Technically, the subject is the part of the sentence about which something is said. The predicate is the part of the sentence that says something about the subject. In the following examples, the subject is in the "S" column and the predicate is in the "P" column.

S	P
Cereal	filled up the bowl.
A striped tiger	sells breakfast cereal.
The little green leprechaun	tossed magically delicious marshmallows into the air.

Subjects and predicates can be broken down further into *complete subjects* and *complete predicates* and *simple subjects* and *simple predicates*. The previous examples show the complete subject and complete predicate of each sentence, as well as examples of a good part of a healthy breakfast.

While the complete subject tells who or what the sentence is about, the simple subject is the noun or pronoun about which something is being said. Here are some examples that identify both complete and simple subjects.

The energetic rabbit blazed across the room to get his hands on some Trix cereal.

Complete Subject: The energetic rabbit
Simple Subject: rabbit

The chocolate Count is my favorite.

Complete Subject: The chocolate Count
Simple Subject: Count

In the complete subjects of the previous sentences, *the* and *energetic* and *the* and *chocolate* are modifiers.

The complete predicate is made up of the verb or verb phrase and its modifiers and complements, which are words or groups of words that complete the meaning of the verb and subject. It's that part of the sentence that tells something about the subject. The simple predicate is the verb or verb phrase. Here are some examples showing both complete and simple predicates:

These new low-sugar cereals increase the need for added sugar.

Complete Predicate: increase the need for added sugar
Simple Predicate: increase

The Frankenberry cereal sank to the bottom of the bowl.

Complete Predicate: sank to the bottom of the bowl
Simple Predicate: sank

In most of your everyday English sentences, the subject comes before the predicate. This follows a logical pattern in speaking and writing. A person usually names what he or she is talking or writing about before he or she expresses the information about it. In some cases, however, we like to mix things up and place predicates before the subjects. The speaker or writer may want to vary sentence construction or add emphasis, or perhaps he's simply drunk out of his gourd, or he's Yoda. In any case, here's an example of what I mean:

Near the bottom of the box waited the secret decoder ring prize.

Identifying the subject can be challenging in sentences like this. There are two strategies you can use. First, find the verb, which in this case is *waited*. Then ask yourself *to whom* or *to what* the verb refers. This word or words will be the subject, and it is *prize*. The second strategy is to rewrite the sentence, reversing the order, as follows:

The secret decoder ring prize waited near the bottom of the box.

Now it's easier to see that *prize* is the subject and *waited* is the verb. Be careful here not to mistake *box* as the subject of the sentence as it was originally written. *Box* is the object of the preposition *of* and therefore can't be the subject of the sentence.

While sentences like the previous example can be written in a way that the verb appears before the subject, an interrogative sentence (aka, a question) is written where the verb always appears before the subject. Say for instance:

Is there any milk in the fridge?

Simple Subject: milk
Simple Predicate: is

Have you seen my special Cheerios spoon?

Simple Subject: you
Simple Predicate: have seen
To find the subject of an interrogative sentence, rewrite the question as a statement to make the subject easier to see.

Milk is in the fridge.
You have seen my special Cheerios spoon.

While the subjects of interrogative sentences usually become apparent when the question is turned into a statement, imperative sentences (aka, commands) can be tricky. In most cases, no subject appears in the sentence. Check out the examples:

Close the refrigerator.

Please open the box.

The verbs, or simple predicates, in these sentences are *close* and *open*, but what are the subjects? In imperative sentences, the person to whom the sentence is directed is almost always *you*. *You* are the one who's being commanded. The subject of these kinds of sentences is *you*. This is true even when *you* doesn't appear in the sentence.

Finding subjects in sentences that begin with *here* or *there* can also be tricky. Although these two words often start sentences, neither one is ever the subject. Note the examples:

There is no Sugar Crisp in the cupboard.

Rewriting this as *No Sugar Crisp is in the cupboard* makes it clear that *Sugar Crisp* is the subject of the sentence. *Is* is the verb.

Here is my spoon.

In this sentence, *spoon* is the subject and *is* is the verb. *Here* serves a special function as an *expletive*, a word that signals that the subject will follow the verb. The pronoun *it* often is used as an expletive as well.

It is difficult chewing when there's so much stupid fiber added to the cereal.

For this sentence, *chewing* is the subject and *is* is the verb.

Finally, the subject of a sentence is never part of a prepositional phrase. Consider the following example:

The trip to the cereal aisle took almost an hour.

Because the noun *aisle* comes right before the verb *took*, some people might think that *aisle* is the subject of the sentence. But the complete predicate *took almost an hour* is not about the *aisle*; it is about *trip*, so *trip* is the subject of the sentence. *Aisle* is in fact the object of the prepositional phrase *to the cereal aisle*. It cannot be the subject of the sentence.

Understanding subjects and predicates is like minding your P's and Q's (well, more like your S's and P's in this scenario). It's not nearly as important as knowing your important breakfast cereals and their associated mascots, but it is essential if you're going to truly understand what makes a sentence a sentence.

Confounded Compound Subjects and Verbs

Along with the many grammatical lessons that we've learned up until now, the most important lesson is that sentences are made up of subjects and verbs (sure we've also learned that paste can be tasty, but it's not really associated with grammar). But what you may not remember from grade school is that subjects and verbs can be either singular or plural, in which case they're generally referred to as being compound. A singular subject refers to one person, place, or thing, and a compound subject refers to two or more simple subjects connected by a conjunction. Likewise, a compound verb refers to two or more verbs or verb phrases connected by a conjunction. This may sound tricky when it's put to you in this sterile descriptive form, but trust me: you'll catch on once I give you these fun-loving examples based on a popular sitcom. Keep in mind that in these examples of compound subjects and verbs, an S indicates a subject and a V indicates a verb.

  S   S   V

Monica and Chandler   are   characters from the show *Friends*.

  S   V   V

Phoebe   danced and sang   her song "Smelly Cat" at Central Perk.

  S   S   V   V

The duck and chicken   quacked and chirped   in Joey's apartment.

  S S   S   V

Carol, Emily, and Rachel are all three of Ross's wives.

  S   V   V

Ross's monkey peed on people and humped their legs.

Compound verbs may also consist of verb phrases, as the following example shows.

> Monica *has started* cleaning and *will continue* cleaning her apartment all day for her annual Thanksgiving Day fiasco.

The verb phrases in this sentence are *has started cleaning* and *will continue*. Connected by the conjunction *and*, they form a compound predicate.

Having a compound subject or compound verb is like getting two or more for the price of one. In most cases compound verbs present little trouble because they flow naturally within the construction of the sentence. Owning a monkey, however, presents a whole lot of trouble and is therefore much more trouble than your basic dog or goldfish.

Super Gerunds: Our Superheroes of Irregular Subjects and Phrases

Okay, here's where things start getting a little bit tricky. Before now, it was pretty darn easy to pick out the subject of a sentence. In most instances it was a noun or a pronoun. But of course, given this wild and whacky language world we live in called English, things don't always follow the norm. And these non-norm subjects are given the non-norm name of a gerund (pronounced JER-und). I know the word "gerund" sounds like something that would be stuck to the bottom of your shoe, but in fact, a gerund actually refers to an irregular subject.

A gerund is like a superhero of grammar. It functions just like an ordinary man on the street, but then, in an instant, it can transform itself into something far more spectacular. For instance, in one form it can be a verb and then, later on, it can become a noun. More precisely, a gerund is a form of a verb that is used as a noun. Here's an example of the power of our grammatical caped crusader:

Swimming is Aquaman's favorite form of exercise.

Swimming is a form of the verb *swim*. In the sentence above, however, it is used as a noun and serves as the subject of the sentence.

A gerund phrase is made up of a gerund and any other words of the phrase. A gerund phrase may contain a single

" This cranky old neighbor I have walked by the other day with her dog and asked me if I would give her dog a pet. I asked if she would rather I give it a kitten or a hamster. She just stood there with that mean look on her face, but I thought the joke was really quite clever. **"**

—Sue

modifying word, a modifying phrase or phrases, or even a clause. Note the following examples:

Quick thinking is a valuable ability in a superhero.

In this sentence, the gerund phrase is *quick thinking*, and the gerund *thinking* is modified by the adjective *quick*.

Flying in a major crime fight requires a superhuman skill.

The gerund phrase is *flying in a major crime fight*, and the gerund *flying* is modified by the prepositional phrase *in a major crime fight*.

Hearing that the Joker had been defeated calmed Gotham City.

The gerund *hearing* is modified by the clause *that the Joker had been defeated*.

Because gerund phrases used as subjects may include several words, the best way to identify them is to find the verb in the sentence. In most cases, a gerund phrase will come directly before a verb. If you find the words that the verb says something about, then these words will likely be the gerund phrase.

A word of caution: A participial phrase (which will be explained in part 3, "The Fine Points about Phrases") is a phrase that acts like an adjective. It may look just like a gerund phrase, but in fact, it's just a cheap imitation and is used in a different manner. Here is an example:

Fighting the evil villains is relaxing.

The gerund phrase is *fighting the evil villains*.

Fighting the evil villains, I relax.

In this sentence, *fighting the evil villains* is a participial phrase. Note that the phrase is set off from the rest of the sentence with a comma. Also note that the subject of the sentence is *I*.

A gerund and a gerund phrase aren't your everyday, regular superheroes of grammar. Knowing that they stem from verbs but can also be used as nouns may seem like a minor point, but grasping the concept shows that you have a solid understanding of the subjects of sentences, and for that, you are worthy of being a grammar superhero!

Chapter 6

mistakes that should not be made on your resume

In this section, we are going to be discussing persons, cases, and pronouns. Before we dive into the depths of the cases and forms of pronouns, let's take a moment to chat about persons. Unfortunately, I'm not referring to gossip, which is a huge disappointment since I find gossip far more interesting than all this grammar crap. I'm talking about persons as in basic terminology that's needed to understand the right usage. Back in high school you may have heard your English teacher talk about terms like "first person singular" or "third person plural" in reference to pronouns. You might have found this talk about persons to be a bit confusing back then, but now that you're a grown-up, or some version thereof, you may have an easier time. Who am I kidding? It still may be a bit confusing, but here goes.

English pronouns have a variety of forms and uses. Pronouns may be singular (I, you) or plural (we, they); they may be masculine (he), feminine (she), or neuter—ouch!—(it).

The *case* of a pronoun is the form it takes to show its grammatical relationship to the words in a sentence. The case of a pronoun may be subjective (also called nominative), objective, or possessive. There. End of lecture. This all may seem like a lot to swallow, so let's look at the different terms one by one. We'll start with the *persons*.

Persons

The person of a pronoun shows the relationship of that pronoun to the speaker of the words. A pronoun may represent the first person, second person, or third person. Each of these persons may be singular or plural, masculine or feminine, or, again ouch, neuter.

The first person refers to the person who is doing the speaking, or even a group of people of which the speaker is a part. Take a look at the example:

I (We) will be there when hell freezes over.

The second person refers to the person or persons spoken to.

You will be there when hell freezes over.

The third person refers to the person or persons (or thing or things) that are spoken about. It's the person or thing that's not the speaker or the person that's spoken to. See for yourself:

He (She, It, They) will be there when hell freezes over.

The third person is sometimes used to refer to a sentence where the subject is given a specific name. The examples that follow, despite not containing a pronoun, are often referred to as a third person construction because *he* can be substituted for *Tom* and *they* can be substituted for *Tom* and *Ann*.

Tom (He) will be there when hell freezes over.

Tom and Ann (They) will be there when hell freezes over.

As my daughter would say, easy peasy!

Cases

Now here comes something that may sound like a mouthful at first, but should become crystal clear by the time we're finished. The case of a pronoun is vital to its correct usage in a sentence. Understanding the cases of pronouns is important because each case has specific uses in a sentence.

Subjective case pronouns are used as subjects or predicate nominatives in a sentence.

Objective case pronouns are used as direct objects, indirect objects, or the objects of a preposition in a prepositional phrase.

Possessive pronouns show ownership or possession.

As you can see, the different cases all have specific uses. I know that's enough to make your hair curl (or straighten, as the case may be), but it's pretty standard when you look at the breakdown of the case forms of the personal pronouns.

Singular Forms

Subjective	Objective	Possessive
First Person		
I	me	my, mine
Second Person		
you	you	your, yours
Third Person		
he, she, it	him, her, it	his, her, hers, its

Plural Forms

Subjective	Objective	Possessive
First Person		
we	us	our, ours
Second Person		
you	you	your, yours
Third Person		
they	them	their, theirs

See? Like I said, once you look at the breakdown, it really is quite easy peasy. In most instances, the correct use of pronouns is obvious, and people don't have much trouble choosing the correct forms. Few people of the over-five crowd would say, "Me went to the store." There are many instances, however, where mistakes are made, one of the most common being with compound subjects, shown in the following example.

Alana and me went to the store. (incorrect)
Alana and I went to the store. (correct)

It's easy to make the mistake shown in the first sentence. In fact, it's more common than picking your nose just as someone enters the room. If you're confused, break up the sentence: "Alana went to the store, and *I* went to the store." Voilà! The first kind of sentence is said all the time in casual conversation but can often slip into formal speaking and writing without the speaker or writer even noticing. Although using the wrong pronouns is one of the most common mistakes of grammar, understanding the various forms and cases of pronouns can help you avoid such mistakes. And leaving your nose alone will help you avoid the other kind of common mistake.

The Grammar Mediator: Making Subjects and Verbs Agree

It's always easier when you agree on things. If you're redoing your bedroom, it's great when you and your significant other agree on how to do it. Unfortunately, in most cases he wants to go with black lacquer and you want a romantic floral look. In Standard English, it's best when things agree as well, especially how subjects and verbs must agree in number. A singular subject refers to one person, place, or thing and requires the singular form of verbs. A plural subject, on the other hand, refers to two or more persons, places, or things and therefore requires the plural form of verbs.

Verb Tenses

Although it's a huge problem when it comes to decorating with spouses, agreement usually isn't a problem for past or future tense verbs (page 104). With the exception of the verb *to be*, English verbs have the same singular and plural forms in the past and future tenses.

Verbs or verb phrases in the present tense, however, offer the most subject-verb agreement problems. Every verb in the present tense, again with the exception of the verb *be*, has two different forms: one form agrees with a singular subject, and the other agrees with a plural subject. Here is an example of the verb *paint* in the past, future, and present tenses in hopes of making this stuff much more mentally palatable:

Past Tense—Singular	Past Tense—Plural
I painted the walls pink last year.	We painted the walls pink last year.
You painted the walls pink last year.	You [All of you] painted the walls pink last year.
He [She, It, or Jack] painted the walls pink last year.	They [Jack and Jill] painted the walls pink last year.

Future Tense—Singular	Future Tense—Plural
I *will paint* the walls pink this year.	We *will paint* the walls pink this year.
You *will paint* the walls pink this year.	You [All of you] *will paint* the walls pink this year.
He [She, It, or Jack] *will paint* the walls pink this year.	They [Jack and Jill] *will paint* the walls pink this year.

Note that regardless of the subject being singular or plural, in the past tense the correct form of the verb remains *painted*, and in the future tense it remains *paint* with the helping verb *will*. But look what happens when we use the present tense.

Present Tense——Singular	Present Tense——Plural
I paint the walls pink.	We paint the walls pink.
You paint the walls pink.	You [All of you] paint the walls pink.
He [She, It, or Jack] paints the walls pink.	They [Jack and Jill] paint the walls pink.

There is one thing you should note here: When the form of the verb *paint* is needed in what's technically known as the third person singular (he, she, it, or Jack) it's *paints* in the present tense, and in all the other singular and plural forms in the present tense it's *paint*.

The present tense singular form of verbs is typically marked with an *–s* or *–es* ending. The plural form of verbs in present tense doesn't end in *–s* or *–es*. Note the following random examples of verbs in present tense:

Verb	Singular	Plural
arrive	arrives	arrive
capture	captures	capture
finish	finishes	finish
grow	grows	grow
imply	implies	imply
perceive	perceives	perceive
say	says	say

An exception to this form is the verb *be*, which has three singular forms for present tense—*am*, *are*, and *is*—but only two forms for past tense, singular and plural—*was* and *were*. Here are examples of the verb *be*:

Present Tense	Past Tense
I am happy with the pink walls.	I was happy with the pink walls.
You are happy with the pink walls.	You were happy with the pink walls.
He [She, It, or Jack] is happy with the pink walls.	He [She, It, or Jack] was happy with the pink walls.
We are happy with the pink walls.	We were happy with the pink walls.
You [All of you] are happy with the pink walls.	You [All of you] were happy with the pink walls.
They [Jack and Jill] are happy with the pink walls.	They [Jack and Jill] were happy with the pink walls.

There are other oddities in the grand scheme, besides of course just painting the walls pink. Except for the verb *be*, the pronoun *I* requires the plural form of verbs in the present tense, despite the fact that *I* is singular. (That is, unless the *I* that you're referring to has some kind of multiple personality disorder.) Consider the following examples:

Singular: I paint little bunnies on the pink wall.

Sue paints little bunnies on the pink wall.

Plural: They paint little bunnies on the pink wall.

It's clear to see who is winning the battle of the bedroom makeover. I hope it's just as clear that the pronoun *you* always requires the plural form of a verb whether the pronoun refers to just one person and is singular or it refers to two or more (like the person with the multiple personality disorder). Below are some examples:

Singular: You [referring to just you] pound the bunnies' heads off with a mallet.

Plural: You [referring to you and a friend] pound the bunnies' heads off with a mallet.

Singular: You [referring to just you] were [not *was*] forced to sleep on the sofa for a week.

Plural: You [referring to you and a friend] were forced to sleep on the sofa for a week.

Just remember this: *Singular nouns* and the pronouns *he*, *she*, and *it* need the singular forms of verbs in the present tense. Plural nouns and the pronouns *I*, *you*, *we*, and *they* require the plural forms of verbs in the present tense. And little bunnies painted on walls require only a little turpentine to remove.

Intervening Phrases

Agreement problems often happen when the subject of a sentence is separated from its verb by an intervening phrase. This can be confusing because a noun in the phrase can be mistaken for the subject of the sentence.

Intervening Prepositional Phrases

The first type of intervening phrases I'll be telling you about are intervening prepositional phrases. If this noun's number is different from the number of the true subject, an agreement mistake can easily be made. Consider the following examples:

The package of rose-patterned bed linens has arrived.

In this sentence, *of rose bed linens* is a prepositional phrase. It's easy to mistake *linens* as the subject of the sentence, which would require the plural helping verb *have*, and which would then make the verb phrase *have arrived*. The true subject, however, is *package*, which is singular. Thus, the verb phrase *has arrived* is correct: *The package has arrived.* Here's another example:

The veto for the dresser's doilies was quick.

In this sentence the prepositional phrase *for the dresser's doilies* separates the singular subject *veto* from the verb *was*. A common mistake with this type of sentence would be to identify *doilies* as the subject of the sentence and change *was* to *were*.

It is essential that you recognize the true subject of a sentence, which is the noun or pronoun the predicate says something about. (Refer back to chapter 2.) In the previous example, the veto was quick; the doilies weren't quick. As you can see, agreement is important in a sentence, as well as in the crucial doily decision.

Parenthetical Phrases

Prepositional phrases aren't the only phrases that can come between a subject and verb, just like doilies aren't the only thing that can come between a marriage. Parenthetical or explanatory phrases that begin with words such as *along with*, *as well as*, *accompanied by*, *in addition to*, *including*, *together with*, or *other than* don't change the number of the subject. Here's an example:

The entire bedroom, including his 1970 black light posters, involves a complete overhaul.

The phrase *including his 1970 black light posters* separates the singular subject *bedroom* from the verb *involves*. The noun *posters*, of course, is plural and would require the plural form of the verb, *involve*. Note that parenthetical or explanatory phrases are often separated from the rest of the sentence by commas. Here's another example:

The husband, along with his buddies Al and Joe, has been instructed to get rid of all of his stuff before his wife returns home from work tonight.

The husband is the subject here, not *Al* and *Joe*. If they were, the helping verb would need to be changed to *have*.

Fractions—The Exception to the Rule

Fractions can cause a problem with agreement as well. When a fraction or a percentage is followed by an intervening phrase, the noun or pronoun of the phrase determines the form of the verb. This goes against the standard rule regarding intervening phrases, which says to ignore the number of nouns or pronouns in the phrase when determining the correct form of the verb. Look at this example:

Two-thirds of the bedroom was left unmoved when she got home because Al and Joe never showed up.

Bedroom, which is the object of the preposition *of*, is singular; therefore the verb *was* is required. Here's another example:

Fifty percent of her vintage spoons were brought into the room.

In this case, *spoons*, which is the object of the preposition, is plural and the verb *were* must be used. Of course since she had her spoon collection, he demanded that he be allowed to bring in fifty percent of his stuffed road kill collection.

Indefinite Pronouns

Indefinite pronouns, when used as subjects, come with their own agreement problems. Indefinite pronouns are pronouns that don't refer to a specific person, place, or thing.

The following indefinite pronouns are usually singular and require the singular form of verbs in the present tense.

anybody	either
anyone	neither
anything	everybody
one	nobody
everyone	somebody
no one	everything
someone	nothing
each	something

Here are some examples:

Each of the lava lamps was tossed yesterday.

Each [lamp] was tossed yesterday.

Note that eliminating the intervening phrase makes it clear that *each* is the singular subject of the sentence.

While some indefinite pronouns are always singular, others are always plural such as, *few, many*, *others*, and *several*. Note the examples:

Several of the lava lamps were ugly.

Several [lamps] were ugly.

Many of the family members object that he has no say in how the new bedroom looks.

Many [members] object that he has no say in how the new bedroom looks.

In the last example, the prepositional phrase *of the family members* separates *many*, which refers to *members* and is the plural subject, from the verb *object*.

As if that weren't confusing enough, while most indefinite pronouns are either singular or plural, some can be singular or plural, depending on the way they're used in a sentence. When words such as *some*, *most*, *all*, *any*, and *none* are used to refer to one thing, they're singular and require the singular form of a verb in the present tense. When they're used to refer to more than one thing, they're plural and require the plural form of the verb. Consider these examples:

> Some of the poodle pillows were hand sewn. (*Some* refers to the plural *pillows* and is therefore plural.)
>
> Some of the poodle pillow was hand sewn. (*Some* refers to the singular *pillow* and is therefore singular.)
>
> All of the flowers in the vase emit a pungent smell. (*All* refers to *flowers* and is plural.)
>
> All emit a pungent smell.
>
> All in the vase emits a pungent smell. (*All* refers to the *vase*, which is a single unit and is singular.)
>
> All emits a pungent smell.

Compound Subjects

Now that we've touched upon singular subjects, let's move on to compound subjects. Don't worry. They're very much the same thing and need to be in agreement with verbs as well. Compound subjects, which refer to two or more persons, places, or things and are joined by the conjunction *and*, usually require the plural form of verbs. It doesn't matter if the individual subjects that make up the compound are singular or plural. If you understood singular subjects, this next stuff should be a breeze. So hold on to the handrails and keep your hands and feet inside the ride at all times. Here we go:

> Bob and Joan are married.
>
> Football and *Desperate Housewives* are both on TV at the same time, causing a big strain in Bob and Joan's marriage.

Few people would think of using *is* instead of *are* in these sentences, and if they were, they wouldn't be doing much thinking at all.

In some sentences, however, a compound subject is considered to be a single unit and not two separate things. In such cases, the singular form of the verb is needed. Check this out:

> Bacon and eggs is Bob's favorite breakfast.

Although *bacon and eggs* makes a compound subject, they are considered to be one item and require the singular verb *is*. Here's another example:

> The Four Corners is the only location in the United States where four states (Arizona, Utah, Colorado, and New Mexico) meet at a single spot, and the only place that Joan wants to go on vacation.

Although *Four Corners* is obviously plural, it refers to one spot. Thus, it requires the singular verb *is*.

Disjunctive Subjects

At first glance, a disjunctive subject may seem to be a compound subject, but there's an important distinction. A disjunctive subject is a subject that consists of two nouns or pronouns that are connected by the conjunctions *or* or *nor*. In a sentence with a disjunctive subject, the verb always agrees with the closer subject. Note the examples:

> Bob or Joan is the head of the family, depending on the situation.

Since the subjects *Bob* and *Joan* are connected by *or*, and since *Joan*, the second subject, is singular and closer to the verb, the verb *is* is required. Note what happens in the next example, though.

> Neither Bob nor his friends play poker on Friday when Joan's book club meets.

The subjects are *Bob* and *his friends*. Because they are connected by *nor*, however, the verb must agree with the closer subject, which is *friends*. Since *friends* is plural, the plural form of the verb *play* is needed. Here's one more example:

> Neither the pedestrians nor the driver was hurt when an angry Bob flew out of the house and drove to the nearest Liquor Barn.

In the example, *pedestrians* and *driver* are the subjects. Although *pedestrians* is plural, the singular *driver* is nearer the verb. Therefore the singular verb *was* is required and not the plural verb *were*.

Collective Nouns

Bob and Joan aren't the only things that have agreement problems. So do collective nouns. Collective nouns, for example, audience, team, committee, jury, flock, and herd, are singular in form (one team or one jury) but in fact represent several members or parts. For instance, there might be fifteen members of a team or eight people in an orgy. (I threw that one in to keep you awake!) Agreement between collective nouns and verbs depends on whether the nouns refer to one thing or many things. Collective nouns need a singular verb when you're thinking of them as a single unit. If you're thinking of the parts or members of the group, the noun requires the plural form of the verb. Note the examples:

> The committee meets after lunch in the mayor's office. (*Committee* here is thought of as one group and requires the singular verb *meets*.)
>
> The jury have not yet reached a verdict. (*Jury* in this sentence refers to the individual members and requires the plural helping verb *have*. Yes, I've been saying it wrong all these years as well.)
>
> The audience was clearly bored with the performance.

(*Audience* refers to everyone in attendance as one group and requires the singular verb *was*. The performance refers to the play *Cats* and explains why they were bored.)

> The audience were applauding and cheering that it was over.

(Here *audience* refers to the individuals and requires the plural verb *were*.)

Nouns in Plural Form

Nouns that are plural in form are similar to collective nouns, but they are generally considered to be singular in meaning. Examples of these nouns include *aeronautics*, *athletics*, *economics*, *mathematics*, *measles*, *news*, *politics*, and *physics*. Because these nouns are singular in meaning, they require the singular forms of verbs. Note the examples:

Mathematics is one of the most important subjects in school even though you rarely get a chance to use it when you grow up.

Politics has always been a heated subject on a date and should never be brought up until there's more heat built up between you.

Be careful, however, if you use one of these nouns to represent individual parts. Consider this example:

The economics of Professor Smith's business model are complex.

In the example, *economics*, the subject of the sentence, refers to various factors of business. It requires the plural verb *are*.

Then, to mix things up a bit, there are nouns that have only plural forms and require plural verbs. For instance, there are nouns like *scissors, pliers,* and *trousers*. The logic behind them needing plural verbs is that scissors have two blades, pliers have two moving parts, and trousers have two legs. In addition, they all end in –*s*, which implies that these words are plural, as the example indicates:

Your trousers are unzipped.

On the other hand, nouns that express quantities or amounts, for example time, money, weight, length, or volume, usually require the singular forms of verbs. Some examples include:

A hundred dollars does not go far anymore.

Five miles is a rather long walk just to clear your head.

Ten gallons of paint is a lot to spill on the new carpet, which I learned the hard way.

Sometimes, however, quantities are considered in individual parts, as in the following example:

Two years have passed since Steve and Janet had sex.

In this case the years are considered to be individual units and require the plural helping verb *have* and not the singular *has*.

Blazing Saddles remains a classic movie among men under thirty.
"Mandy" is a Barry Manilow favorite with women over forty.

Once in a while you may find a sentence where a singular subject is connected by way of a linking verb to a plural complement, or you may find the opposite in which a plural subject is linked to a singular complement. (For more about complements, see "Complimenting Complements" in the upcoming chapter, page 125.) In these cases, the linking verb should agree with the subject, such as in the following example:

An all-time favorite of divorce lawyers is spousal debates.

The subject of the sentence is *favorite*, the linking verb is *is*, and the complement is *debates*. *Favorite* is singular and *debates* is plural; however, the verb must agree with *favorite*.

❝ I needed shelves hung and got the name of a good handyman. He was great with tools but horrible with grammar and would say things like 'these pliers is new.' I thought I was being helpful correcting him, but he stopped returning my calls. I learned an important lesson: having a handyman that can build shelves is more important than having a handyman that can build a proper sentence. **❞**

—Jake

Here's another example.

They are a happy family.

The subject *they* is plural and requires the plural linking verb *are*. The complement *family* is singular, but the verb must agree with *they*.

 Special note: *The titles of creative works such as books, stories, TV shows, movies, songs, paintings, and sculptures require the singular forms of verbs even when the title is in plural form. The title refers to one thing, as the examples show.*

Expletives (No, Not Swear Words)

A final possible agreement problem is the sentence beginning with the expletives *here* or *there* and a form of the verb *be*. In these kinds of sentences you have to make sure that you identify the subject correctly and select the correct form of the verb. Also, you have to pay close attention to contractions, because it's common to mess things up. Here are some examples:

There are three pairs of women's underpants in Bob's glove compartment.

In this sentence, *pairs* is the subject and *are* is the correct form of the verb. Now consider the following:

There's three pairs of women's underpants in Bob's glove compartment.

To many people this may sound acceptable, but it's incorrect. (It's also not very acceptable that Bob has three pairs of women's underwear in his glove compartment. Sure, they *could* belong to Joan, but I think we've all seen enough Lifetime movies to know that's highly unlikely.) But back to the sentence at hand, the contraction *There's*, which means *there is*, is not the right way to say that sentence. *Is* agrees with the singular *pair*, but not with *pairs*. The verb should be *are*, and the sentence should be written *There are* . . . or the less common, *There're*. Or Bob could ditch two of the pairs so we could write, *There is a pair of women's underpants in his glove compartment.*

Agreement between subjects and verbs is a topic that can aggravate the most meticulous speaker and writer. But it's these minor rules that can leave a major impression when not followed correctly. So strap on your overalls and get to work. (Man, I guess I need a bit of work in this department myself!)

Chapter 7

putting the pieces together

Now that you've finished cleaning your head wound and had a stiff drink to numb the pain, let's move on to the next step in understanding grammar. This next step is to learn just how the various pieces of this glorious little puzzle we call the English language fit together. If you think about it, the order that subjects, verbs, and complements take in a sentence results in patterns. These patterns help ensure that the ideas we're trying to communicate come off logically and clearly—or at least they will once the effects of the stiff drink wear off.

Sentence Patterns—Putting the Pieces Together

As complex and varied as English sentence construction may seem at first, just know that all sentences in the English language actually follow a few basic patterns. If you understand these patterns, then you can avoid building sentences that don't have a strong foundation and that will get marked up with a red pen once your teacher gets a hold of them.

The most basic sentence pattern is the subject-verb pattern. In the subject-verb pattern, the verb must be an action verb or a verb that expresses a state of being. Linking verbs don't count and are a part of other sentence patterns. Here are some examples of the basic subject-verb sentence pattern, which, for your entertainment value, will continue with the enjoyable theme of bodily injury:

S	V
Arms	break.
Kidneys	fail.

Modifiers don't affect sentence patterns. No matter how many modifiers a subject or verb may have, the basic pattern remains. Just take a look:

S	V	
The infected wound	bled	steadily throughout the night.

In a sentence pattern, a verb phrase is considered a simple verb. The verb phrase in the following example is underlined.

S	V	
Jason	had been limping	all day.

Compound elements don't change sentence patterns either. Consider these examples:

S		S	V	
Jake	and	Amy	went	to the hospital together.

	S	V	V	
The victims	ate	and	drank	the rancid hospital food for days.

	S		S	V		V
The hand	and	wrist	snapped	and	broke on impact.

Basic sentence patterns also don't change with interrogative sentences or sentences that are inverted. Here, check it out for yourself:

	V	S	V	
Where	did	Ken	fall? (The verb phrase is *did fall*.)

	V		S
Out of the plane wreck	walked	the injured.

If you suddenly want to take a break and watch an episode of *ER*, I understand. But try to focus a bit longer until I finish explaining all the various sentence patterns. The next sentence pattern is a bit more complicated. Okay, it's a lot more complicated. Or at least it sounds like it is. But as usual, the examples are tremendously helpful in making things more clear. This next sentence pattern is the subject–linking verb–predicate nominative pattern. Remember that a predicate nominative is a noun or pronoun that follows a linking verb and renames the subject. Examples:

S	LV	PN	
Christina	was	my roommate	at Belleview Hospital.

S	LV	PN	
Riley	is	a patient	in ICU.

Another sentence pattern is the (now take a big breath for this one) subject–linking verb–predicate adjective pattern. Remember that a predicate adjective, which must be an adjective, modifies the subject of a sentence. Note the examples:

S	LV	PA	
Dr. Leon	was	meticulous	when sewing Jim's thumb back on his hand.

S	LV	PA	
The wound	was	gaping,	well over five inches.

	S	LV	PA
During the splenectomy,	the patient	was	terrified.

Another common sentence pattern is the subject–verb–direct object pattern (sounds a bit like the hokey pokey of grammar). A direct object receives the action of a verb, as the following examples show:

S	V	DO	
My sister	watches	surgery	shows	on TV.

S	V	DO	DO	DO
Josh	broke	his arm,	leg,	and nose.

Along with a direct object, a sentence may have an indirect object. This results in another common sentence pattern. An indirect object identifies *for whom* or *to whom* the action of a verb is done. Sentences with an indirect object have a subject–verb–indirect object–direct object pattern. A mouthful, I know, but note the examples:

S	V	IO	DO
Luke	gave	Janice	the Heimlich maneuver.

S	V	IO	DO
Janice	gave	Luke	a kiss	for saving her life.

Still another sentence pattern is the subject–verb–direct object–objective complement pattern (I'll give you a sec to let that one sink in). An objective complement describes the direct object and usually follows a direct object, but it can only be used with a few action verbs (see "Complimenting Complements" below). Here are some examples:

S	V	DO	OC
The doctors	elected	Tom	chief-of-staff.

No matter how complicated a sentence may look with all those modifiers, phrases, and clauses, all sentences are built on the basic patterns described above. Consider the

following examples of a compound, complex, and compound-complex sentence:

S	V	S
The terrible fever	raged	through the night, but by morning

S	LV	PA
the patient	felt	better.

	S				V
Although	Bill,	feeling awful about firing the gun,			sent

IO	DO	S	V	DO	
Denise	roses,	she	returned	the flowers	to him.

	S	V		S	V
As	she	lay	in her bed,	Tara	watched

	DO			S	V
the skin-eating bacteria	on her arm, and			she	thought	of home.

Understanding sentence patterns may strike some people
as being overly technical in learning basic grammar. Who
really needs to know sentence patterns anyway as long as
they can put a decent sentence together? While it's true that
a person can construct a sentence without knowing the basic
sentence patterns, the person who does understand them
will have a better overall grasp of communicating, both in
speaking and writing.

Think of it this way. You can be playing poker against
someone who knows the basic rules of the game. Or you can
be playing against a person who knows and understands not

just the basics but all the rules, the strategies, and the words
to Kenny Rogers's "The Gambler." Over the long run, whom
do you think you'll fare better against?

Complimenting Complements

English would be a lot simpler, and this book would be a
lot shorter, if every sentence consisted of only a subject and
a verb. But as luck would have it, most sentences contain a
third element, a *complement*. What complements do is embellish sentences by adding information. Here's an example of
what I mean:

Tom plays.

Okay, Tom plays, but what does he play? Baseball?
Cards? Parcheesi? The field? By adding the complement
accordion, we enrich the sentence and complete the thought
more thoroughly.

Tom plays the accordion.

Although *the accordion* is a *complement*, it's not really much
of a *compliment* to Tom since a guy who plays the accordion
is definitely not a chick magnet. As you can see, a complement (note the spelling with the *e*, complement) is a word
or group of words that elaborates or completes the meaning
of a subject or predicate. There are several different kinds of
complements that we'll learn about in this chapter, including: predicate nominatives, predicate adjectives, direct
objects, indirect objects, and objective complements.

Predicate Nominatives and Adjectives

The first kind of complement, a *predicate nominative*, is a noun or pronoun that follows a linking verb. (Remember that linking verbs are forms of the verb *be* [*am, are, is, was, were, be, being*], all verb phrases ending in *been* or *be*, and *become, seem, grow, appear, look, feel, smell, taste, remain, sound*, and *stay*.) A predicate nominative renames the subject. I know. This always sounds so confusing until I show you an example and then you hit your forehead with the heel of your palm and say, "Oh yeah, now I get it." So here goes. Here are some examples of a predicate nominative, in which the subjects are labeled S, the linking verbs are labeled LV, and the predicate nominatives are labeled PN:

S	LV	PN
Harriet	is	an accountant.

S	LV	PN
Mosquitoes	are	nasty bloodsuckers.

S	LV	PN	PN	
Tom	was	a drummer	and motorcyclist	for several years.

There. Are you hitting yourself yet? In these examples, notice that predicate nominatives, as well as all other complements, can be compound. Also note that Harriet sounds like a perfect match for Tom, who, might I add, enjoys bad boy hobbies like playing the drums and riding motorcycles to counteract his love of the accordion. But, back to grammar. Like other complements, predicate nominatives can't be a part of a prepositional phrase. In the last example, *for several years* is a prepositional phrase. Even though *years* is a noun, *years* can't be a complement, since it's the object of the preposition *for*.

Unlike a predicate nominative, which must be a noun or pronoun, a *predicate adjective* is, yes, you guessed it, an adjective. It follows a linking verb and modifies the subject of a sentence. In the following examples, the predicate adjectives are labeled PA:

S	LV	PA	
Tina	was	happy	with her acceptance to college.

S	LV	PA
The hikers	appeared	exhausted.

S	LV	PA		PA
The puppy	is	adorable	and	lovable.

You're doing it again, aren't you? You're smacking yourself in the forehead? I knew it! Let's continue. Sometimes predicate nominatives and predicate adjectives are grouped together and called *subject complements*. This is because the complements refer to the subject of a sentence . . . duh.

Direct and Indirect Objects

Whereas predicate nominatives and predicate adjectives are used only with linking verbs, direct objects and indirect objects are used with action verbs.

A *direct object* is a word or words that receive the action of a verb. They can be nouns, pronouns, phrases, or clauses, and they usually answer the questions *whom?* or *what?* In the following examples, direct objects are labeled DO.

S	V	DO
Beth	visited	her brother.

(The DO is a noun.)

S	V	DO	
Patricia	called	him	about the project.

(The DO is a pronoun.)

S	V	DO
Darrin	enjoys	*listening to music.*

(The DO is a phrase.)

S	V	DO
Most people	realize	*that traffic delays are inevitable.*

(The DO is a clause.)

S	V	DO		DO
Marty	likes	football	and	baseball.

(The DOs are nouns. This is also a case of compound direct objects.)

Let's move on to indirect objects. Before we do, you may want to revisit chapter 1, when life, and grammar, were easier, to brush up on the difference between transitive and intransitive verbs. Here's where things get a bit tricky, but if you really concentrate, you should be okay. While a direct object receives the action of the verb, an *indirect object* is a word that identifies *for whom* or *to whom* the action of the verb is done. Also, an indirect object usually comes before the direct object. To have an indirect object, a sentence must have a direct object, but a sentence with a direct object doesn't need to have an indirect object. See, I told you it's confusing. Read it again if you'd like. I'll wait. . . . Great. Here are some examples. Note that I labeled indirect objects as IO to help you out a bit. You're welcome.

S	V	IO	DO	
The salesperson	showed	us	a new car.	

S	V	IO	DO	
I	handed	Caryn	her car keys.	

S	V	IO	DO	
Maria	gave	Oliver	a watch	for his birthday.

A word to the wise. Be careful not to mistake words that are in a prepositional phrase for an indirect object. Prepositions such as *to* or *for* are signals that the following noun or pronoun is the object of the preposition and not the indirect object. Like in the following examples:

S	V	IO	DO
Danielle	gave	him	the list.

S	V	DO	
Danielle	gave	the list	to him.

In the second example, *to him* is a prepositional phrase in which *him* is the object of the preposition *to*. *Him* is not an indirect object.

Objective Complements

We're just about done here. The final kind of complement is called an objective complement. An *objective complement* follows a direct object and describes the object. A sentence must have a direct object in order to have an objective complement. Objective complements only follow a select few action verbs, noted on the following page:

- appoint
- choose
- consider
- elect
- find
- make
- name
- prove
- think
- voted

In the examples that follow, objective complements are labeled OC.

S	V	DO	OC
The committee	named	Sam	liaison.

S	V	DO	OC
Erica	considers	David	a friend.

S	V	DO	OC
The rough seas	made	Jessie	queasy.

If all of this is still not sinking in, what I'm really trying to tell you is that complements enrich sentences and better enable you to give more information to your listeners and readers. Sure, they can be a pain in the ass to understand when you dissect the heck out of them like the way we just did, but they are important elements of sentences and you should know a thing or two about them. This is especially true if you play the accordion, since maybe your knowledge of grammar will counteract that and help you attract chicks.

Chapter 8

miscellaneous maladies

There are three sins in life that we're all guilty of committing. One, telling someone that we've already mailed a letter when we know full well that it's still sitting on our dining room table. Two, canceling a dentist appointment less than twenty-four hours in advance by saying that there's been a death in the family so that we won't be charged. And three, using poor grammar when it comes to the subjective case of a pronoun.

On the Subject of Subjective Case Pronouns

To help you avoid at least one of these errors, I must begin by saying a confusing sentence: The subjective case of a pronoun is used when the pronoun is the subject of a sentence or clause or a predicate nominative (also known as a subject complement). The following are the subjective case pronouns:

Singular	Plural
First Person	
we	they
Second Person	
you	you
Third Person	
he, she, it, who, whoever	they, who, whoever

You should note that only the pronouns listed above can be used as the subjects or predicate nominatives of a sentence. Also note that although the dreaded *who* and *whoever* aren't personal pronouns, they can function as subjective case pronouns as well. The same form is used for both singular and plural. (*Who* and *whom* are discussed in further detail in chapter 9.)

There, now that you're as confused as trying to remember which way to set the clocks for Daylight Savings Time, let me try to simplify things. One of the most common mistakes that is made with pronouns is not using a subjective form as the subject of a compound sentence. In fact, committing this error is more common than . . . well, than setting the clocks the wrong way for Daylight Savings Time. For instance, I'm sure that you've commonly referred to those who are traveling to a far off and distant land as the following:

> Her and Jay went to Madagascar.
>
> Kerrie and me went to Madagascar.
>
> The Smiths and us went to Madagascar.

First problem: It's wrong that in each of these sentences, a pronoun other than a subjective case pronoun is used as a subject. Second problem: It's wrong that other people get to travel to such exotic places when the most exotic place I've traveled to in years is IKEA. Here are the corrected versions of the above sentences:

> She and Jay went to Madagascar.
> Kerrie and I went to Madagascar.
> The Smiths and we went to Madagascar.

And to solve the other wrongdoing, I must book myself on an exotic vacation right away. But don't worry. Before I go, I want to enlighten you as to an easy trick that will stop those grammatical mistakes in their tracks. There's a simple test that you can do that will help you determine the correct form of pronouns to use as subjects. Simply use each subject separately with the verb of the sentence or clause. It'll then be obvious which form to use. Consider the examples again.

> Her went to Madagascar. (incorrect)
> She went to Madagascar. (correct)
> Me went to Madagascar. (incorrect)
> I went to Madagascar. (correct)
> Us went to Madagascar. (incorrect)
> We went to Madagascar. (correct)

If you take the compound subjects apart and use each with the verb, it can help you to recognize the correct pronoun to use. It's a simple but effective method for making sure that you're using correct grammar. Oh if only all problems in life were so easy to fix.

Another common mistake with subjective case pronouns is to use an incorrect form as a predicate nominative. Remember that a predicate nominative is a noun or pronoun that follows a linking verb and renames the subject of a sentence. This is why a pronoun, when used as a predicate nominative, must be a subjective case pronoun. Here's what I mean in this common, although, incorrect sentence:

This is *her* speaking.

Using subjective case pronouns, the sentence is corrected:

This is *she* speaking.

Yes, it will sound a bit strange when someone calls and asks, "Is Jill there?" and you answer "This is she" (especially when your name's not Jill), but at least it will be grammatically correct.

Yet another construction that can result in errors occurs when pronouns are paired with a noun, for example *us guys* or *we patriots*. Note the examples and decide which is correct:

Us vegetarians believe in not eating anything that once had a face.
We vegetarians believe in not eating anything that once had a face.

Most people would say that each sounds okay, but only one is correct. Here again, a simple test will help you to rec-

“ My friend Nancy is proud of the fact that she says, 'this is she' when someone asks for her on the phone. She thinks she comes across sounding educated but I guarantee people think she sounds like an idiot. **”**

—Janice

ognize the correct form. Drop the noun and use the pronoun alone in each sentence.

Us believe in not eating anything that once had a face. (incorrect)

We believe in not eating anything that once had a face. (correct)

We vegetarians believe in not eating anything that once had a face. (correct)

Of course, there are exceptions. In informal conversation it's acceptable to use *It is me* or *It's me*. Because language and expression are constantly evolving and changing, someday these short sentences may even be acceptable in Standard English. For now, though, when speaking or writing in a formal setting, sticking with Standard English (*It is I*) is the better choice.

The Object of Objective Case Pronouns

Here we go again. But instead of talking about subjective cases, now we're going to chat a bit about objective cases. Words that function as objects of an action verb or a preposition are in the objective case. Therefore, objects require the objective case of personal pronouns.

The object of a verb is like a reporter for the *National Inquirer* and answers the question *what?* or *whom?* An object of a verb may be a direct object or an indirect object.

Note the objective case pronouns:

Singular	Plural
First Person	
me	us

Singular	Plural
Second Person	
you	you
Third Person	
him, her, it	them
whom, whomever	whom, whomever

Just so we're clear, only the pronouns above can be used as the objects of verbs or prepositions. Although *whom* and *whomever* aren't personal pronouns, they can function as objective case pronouns; as you can see, the same form is used for both singular and plural. (For those of you who are unsure about the usage of *who* and *whom*—and who isn't—they are addressed in chapter 9.)

Few people have trouble with singular objects. Most realize right away that sentences like *Sue gave I the book*, or *Sue gave the book to he* are grammatically incorrect. The problem arises when objective pronouns come from compound objects. Consider the following type of incorrect example, which is a sentence that you've no doubt even said before (assuming of course that you have friends named Bridgette and Tom, and you all need directions).

> Bridgette sent Tom and I different instructions.

You can use that simple trick I taught you before to see if it's correct. As with subjective case pronouns, using each pronoun separately in the sentence will help you to easily select the correct form.

> Bridgette sent I different instructions. (incorrect)
> Bridgette sent me different instructions. (correct)

Bridgette sent Tom and me different instructions. (correct)

It really is a great trick, huh? It's far more useful than the one where you pat your head with one hand and circle your belly with the other.

As you can see, using each object in the sentence separately clearly shows that *I* is incorrect and should be replaced with *me*. *I* is a subjective case pronoun and *me* is an objective case pronoun.

Like the objects of verbs, the pronouns that function as objects of prepositions must also be in the objective case. Just so we're clear, the object of a preposition is the last word or words in a prepositional phrase (which we covered in chapter 2). Once again, compound objects, and especially when the pronoun *I* is a part of the compound object, can be the cause of mistakes. Consider the following example:

This éclair is for you and I.

As you can see, this is only an example since I never ever share my éclairs. Given that, the prepositional phrase in the sentence is *for you and I*. The word *for* is the preposition and *you* and *I* are the objects. *I*, however, is a subjective case pronoun and can't be used as an object—unless of course you like sounding like you're uneducated and striving for a job at a waste plant. The correct pronoun is *me*, as the following example shows.

This éclair is for you and me.

Here's a similar, and commonly incorrect, prepositional phrase.

Between you and I, I could eat the éclair all by myself.

In this sentence, *Between you and I* is a prepositional phrase. *Between* is the preposition, and *you and I* are the objects. Don't be fooled by the fact that the phrase begins the sentence and think that *I* is part of a compound subject (*you* and *I*) and is therefore correct. The objects of a prepositional phrase can never be subjects of a sentence. As objects of the preposition, the pronouns *you* and *me* are required. Thus:

Between you and me, I could eat the éclair all by myself.

Just like with subjective case pronouns, mistakes with objective case pronouns often occur when pronouns are paired with nouns. Here's an example:

Our parents don't understand we kids.

And neither do their English teachers for that matter, but that's beside the point. The above sentence is just plain wrong, because a subjective case pronoun, *we*, is used when the objective case pronoun, *us*, is needed. Dropping the noun makes the correct form clear.

Our parents don't understand we. (incorrect)
Our parents don't understand us. (correct)
Our parents don't understand us kids. (correct)

Objective case pronouns serve as objects in a sentence. They can be nothing more and they are nothing less. Learning to distinguish subjective and objective case pronouns will help you to avoid using these words incorrectly in speaking and writing. You'll be a lot better off if you just use that nifty trick I taught you.

66 I was taking a break from studying and I turned on my soap. I heard these two characters say 'between you and I' and I realized that if the FCC would stop paying so much attention to how violence on TV affects kids and start caring about the effects of bad grammar, the world would be a much more grammatically correct place in which to live. **99**

—Alexis

More Positively Possessive Pronouns

When it comes right down to it, we're all greedy little pigs. Even those billionaire celebrities that clamor over free Oscar baskets as if they were wedding dresses at Filene's Basement's annual sale. Possessive pronouns are no exception. Possessive pronouns are actually personal pronouns that show possession, or ownership. In the sentence Orlando Bloom forgot his free Cartier watch, for instance, *his* is a possessive case pronoun indicating that the bling-bling belongs to Orlando.

The important thing to know about possessive case pronouns is that they do not require an apostrophe. This is quite different from nouns, which require apostrophes to show possession such as: *Orlando's Cartier watch*. You can put this rule in the file with all the other little quirks of English, like "*i* before *e* except after *c*," but it's an important point to remember because it will help you to avoid mistakes down the line.

Anyone that's been through a divorce is quite experienced in possessive pronouns because they've gone through a lot of emotional upheaval and high legal bills to determine some of the most common ones: yours and mine. But for

those who haven't, here are some more examples of possessive pronouns:

Singular	Plural
First Person	
my, mine	our, ours
Second Person	
your, yours	your, yours
Third Person	
his, her, hers, its	their, theirs
whose	whose

Note that *whose*, a variation of *who*, is a possessive form
(not to be confused with *who's*, which is a contraction for *who
is*). The same form is used for both singular and plural.

Some possessive pronouns replace a noun and can stand
alone. Others are used with nouns in sentences. Here's the
breakdown:

> **Stand Alone:** mine, his, yours, hers, ours, theirs
>
> **Used with Nouns:** my, your, his, her, its, our, their

As you can see from the lists, *his* can stand alone or be
used with a noun, as the examples show:

> *That car is his,* since he bought it before we got married.
> *That is his car,* but it will soon be mine after the divorce.

Similarly, depending upon the construction, *whose* can
stand alone or be used with nouns.

Whose laptop is that?

Whose is that?

Gerunds

In most instances, choosing the right possessive case pronoun doesn't present much trouble. However, using possessive case pronouns with a gerund or gerund phrase can be confusing, especially since the majority of you have no doubt forgotten what a gerund is by now anyway. To review gerunds and gerund phrases, return to chapter 5, but in the meantime, here are two examples, in which the gerunds are italicized:

Her *dancing* was just a wee bit better than Elaine's dancing on *Seinfeld*.

His *singing* at the party was just a wee bit better than that of William Hung, the *American Idol* reject.

In the two examples, *her* and *his* possess the gerunds. They also possess knowledge as to why this couple is divorcing. The possessive case of the pronouns is therefore necessary. Following are examples of what should be a possessive case pronoun modifying a gerund phrase. The phrase is italicized. Choose which sentence is correct.

Him *working all hours of the night* became a strain.

His *working all hours of the night* became a strain.

Him is often used in this type of construction; however, *him* is an objective case pronoun. It's not correct in this sentence. It's also not correct in a marriage to be such a workaholic. Grammatically speaking, a possessive case pronoun is required, which means *his* is correct. Matrimonially, a legal case is required, which means a divorce.

Contractions

Another all-too-common error with some possessive case pronouns is to confuse the possessive pronouns with contractions. Note the following list of possessive pronouns, contractions, and the words that make up the contractions:

Possessive Pronoun	Contraction
its	it's (it is)
your	you're (you are)
their	they're (they are)
whose	who's (who is)

To avoid using contractions in place of possessive case pronouns, as well as to avoid using possessive case pronouns in place of contractions, remember that possessive pronouns don't have apostrophes and that contractions are shortened forms of words. Still, if you find yourself wondering if you're using these words correctly, you can test them in a sentence. Here are some examples:

> The divorce decree stayed in *it's* envelope.
> The divorce decree stayed in *its* envelope.

Its and *it's* are often used incorrectly. To check which sentence is correct, turn the contraction into its original words, *it is*, and substitute these words for the contraction in the sentence. The first sentence then becomes the following:

> The divorce decree stayed in *it is* envelope.

Obviously, this is wrong. Here's another example:

Who's lace g-string is that?
Whose lace g-string is that?

Turn *who's* to *who is* and substitute these words for *who's* in the sentence.

Who *is* lace g-string is that?

As you can see, that's wrong. *Whose* should start the sentence. It's also wrong to play mattress tag when the divorce isn't final, but let's stick to the matter at hand. Because it's so easy to mix up these pronouns and contractions, here's one more example:

The Petersons keep their boat at the marina.
The Petersons keep they're boat at the marina.

Turn *they're* back to *they are* and use the words for *they're* in the sentence.

The Petersons keep *they are* boat at the marina.

Again, it's clear which form is correct. What may not be as clear is that if Mr. Peterson wants to keep his hands on his boat, he has to move that sucker to a hidden location until after the divorce is finalized.

One final note. Pay especially close attention when using the possessive case pronoun *their*, not only for misusing it with *they're*, but also for misusing it with *there*. You've no doubt seen sentences like the following:

The closet is over their. (incorrect)

The closet is over there. (correct)

The locks to there house were changed. (incorrect)

The locks to their house were changed. (correct)

Understanding the forms of possessive case pronouns can help you to avoid mistakes in their usage. Understanding that being a workaholic isn't conducive to a good marriage can help you avoid mistakes in marriage number two.

The Antecedent: The Brownnoser of Grammar

Every corporate job has them: a gopher who tails behind his high-power boss and agrees with every little thing that the boss says. These weaklings don't speak their mind or challenge authority. Instead, they trot around all day saying the two subordinate words, "yes, sir." The English language has this same kind of brownnoser, and it is called an antecedent. That's because an antecedent spends its whole life forever agreeing with a pronoun.

As you may remember from pages back, a pronoun is a word that takes the place of a person, place, thing, or idea. The word, or words, a pronoun refers to is called its *antecedent*.

Here's a brief example for review:

Tom went to the ATM because he was out of money.

The pronoun, of course, is *he*, and the antecedent is *Tom*. Pronouns must agree in number and gender with their antecedents. This means that a singular antecedent (*man*) calls for a singular pronoun (*him*), and a plural antecedent (*people*) calls for a plural pronoun (*they*). Likewise, a masculine antecedent (*Lance*) requires a masculine pronoun (*he*);

a feminine antecedent (*Alexis*) requires a feminine pronoun (*her*); and a neuter antecedent (*rock*) requires a neuter pronoun (*it*). Note the following examples of pronouns and their antecedents in the underground world of televised crime:

> *Tony Soprano* manages *his* family's business. (singular, masculine)
>
> *Carmela* can't find *her* stacks of cash hidden in the compost heap. (singular, feminine)
>
> The bullet-ridden *corpse* came down with a crash, but *it* missed the river. (singular, neuter)
>
> The *boys* packed *their* guns for the next big hit. (plural)

As a general rule, use the pronouns *he*, *him*, or *his* with a singular, masculine antecedent. For singular, feminine antecedents use *she*, *her*, or *hers*. For antecedents that are neuter use *it* or *its*. Plural pronouns are not sensitive to gender. In the plural example above, the antecedent *boys* could be replaced with *girls* without having to change the pronoun *their*.

When two or more antecedents are joined by *and*, they form a compound antecedent and require a plural pronoun. This is true even if the antecedents are both singular. Note the examples:

> *Tony* and *Carmela* enjoyed *their* vacation in the Cayman Islands visiting their money.
>
> *Christopher* and *the mob* enjoyed planning *their* next money-laundering scheme.

When two or more antecedents are joined by *or* or *nor*, the pronoun should agree with the closest antecedent. This, of course, isn't a problem when the two antecedents are singular, like they are in the following example:

Either *Junior* or *Silvio* plans to bring *his* pistols to A. J.'s graduation party.

This rule also works well with two plural antecedents or when a singular antecedent comes before a plural one, as the next example shows:

Neither *Adrianna* nor the other *girlfriends* support *their* boyfriends' desires to go out with strippers.

In this case, the plural pronoun *their* agrees with the plural noun *girlfriends*. If the antecedents are reversed, however, the sentence becomes unclear and somewhat awkward.

Neither the other *girlfriends* nor *Adrianna* supports *her* boyfriends.

Since the pronoun must agree with the nearest antecedent, which is *Adrianna*, the pronoun *her* is necessary. But this causes a problem with *girlfriends*, which is plural. It also makes the sentence unclear. Does the sentence mean that the girlfriends won't support Adrianna's boyfriends? Or are the boyfriends the girlfriends' boyfriends too? As you can see, this sentence is as confusing as how someone can live a life of crime and sleep well at night. In any case, reworking the sentence in the form of the first example, in which the plural antecedent is positioned second and using the pronoun *their*, will make it much more logical.

When used as antecedents, indefinite pronouns may result in agreement problems as well. Several indefinite pronouns—for example *anyone*, *each*, *either*, *everything*, *neither*, *none*, *no one*, *nothing*, *someone*, and *something*—are almost always singular and require singular pronouns. Note the following examples:

Nothing was where *it* should be after the "family" came over for Sunday dinner.

Neither of the hit men had *his* gun holster on when they went out for the hit.

Other indefinite pronouns—for example, *all*, *any*, *more*, *most*, *none*, and *some*—can be singular or plural, depending on their use in a sentence. Consider the examples:

None of the FBI's surveillance equipment was as sophisticated as we expected *it* to be.

None of the bodies found along the river had *their* own blocks of cement tied to *their* waists.

Occasionally, indefinite pronouns, which are usually singular, may be used in a collective sense. This makes them function as a plural. Here's an example of just what the heck I'm talking about:

Everybody used *their* fake IDs when jetting off to Vegas for the annual Mafia conference.

For sentences like this, agreement may be made more precise by rewriting the sentence as follows:

The "family" members used their fake IDs when jetting off to Vegas for the annual Mafia conference.

Agreement in such cases can also be made more precise by writing two singular pronouns. The combination, *his or her*, can take the place of the plural *their*, although this can, depending on the sentence, be somewhat wordy as the following example shows:

Everyone used his or her fake ID when jetting off to Vegas for the annual Mafia conference.

Collective nouns may also be singular or plural, depending on their intended use in a sentence. Pronouns should be chosen accordingly. Note the examples:

> The audience clapped and stood to show *its* approval of the play about plastic horse heads.
>
> The audience *members* clapped and stood to show *their* approval of the play about plastic horse heads.

A significant issue with indefinite pronouns and antecedents is sexist usage. Sexism is a huge problem in today's society anyhow, so it makes sense that it's permeated into the walls of grammar. In the past, singular masculine pronouns were used to agree with antecedents when the antecedent was an indefinite singular pronoun. Here's an example of a sentence that's still commonly used today:

> *Everyone* is responsible for *his* own actions.

Everyone is a singular indefinite pronoun, which might refer to a man or woman. *His*, however, is masculine. The consensus these days is that such constructions are sexist, since they ignore the possibility that *everyone* can refer to a woman as well as a man.

This problem extends to noun antecedents for which we don't know the gender. Here are two examples:

> A business *owner* must be attentive to *his* customers.
>
> A *teacher* must be observant of the needs of *his* students.

In each sentence, the antecedent certainly might refer to a woman, especially since women can be both teachers as well as business owners. Therefore, the sentence might be considered to be insensitive to women.

There are a couple of easy methods you can use to avoid this issue, and future sexual lawsuits. For one thing, you can use the construction *he or she* or *his or her*. For example:

> Everyone is responsible for *his or her* own accommodations.
>
> A business owner must be attentive to *his or her* customers.

Another way to avoid sexism in sentences is to alternate the use of the pronouns *he* and *she* throughout the written material or conversation. This can tend to be confusing to the reader or listener, however, since the genders change more often than they do in *Victor/Victoria*. Instead, you might want to rework such sentences to the plural, which doesn't identify gender, such as in the following examples:

> People are responsible for *their* own accommodations.
>
> Business *owners* must be attentive to *their* customers.
>
> *Teachers* must be observant of the needs of *their* students.

The method you choose to use will depend on the material, the construction, and whether you have any Mafia leaders after you. You should choose the method that's easiest for your listeners or readers to understand, and that best expresses your ideas.

Chapter 9

who needs to know?

It's time to discuss that part of the book that I've been warning you about. The one that will teach you all about the intricacies of those two tricksters of the English language: *who* and *whom*. This dastardly duo of pronouns are responsible for more confusion than the transgender movement of the early 1980s.

To Who or Not to Whom, That Is the Question

The team of who and whom actually have dual use. They may be used as interrogative pronouns, which ask a question, or as relative pronouns, which introduce a subordinate clause in a sentence. The pronouns are actually a single pronoun in two different cases. Who is a subjective case pronoun; whom is an objective case pronoun. Whoever and whomever are variations of who and whom and follow the same rules in regard to case and use. Just remembering the different uses for subjective and objective case pronouns can help you to use these two confounding words correctly.

But as confusing as these two ponderous pronouns can be, there is no reason to worry your pretty little head. For once again, I'm here for you and will teach you a simple trick of the trade that will help you determine which pronoun to use. Since *who* is a subjective case pronoun, it can be used in the same types of constructions that *he*, *she*, and *they* can. (*He*, *she*, and *they* are subjective case pronouns.) Since *whom* is an objective case pronoun, it can be used in the same types of constructions that *him*, *her*, and *them* can. (These are objective case pronouns.) There! Simple, isn't it?

Let's put the test to work. Consider the examples and decide which of each pair is correct.

Who called last night?

Whom called last night?

Who or *whom* is the subject of the example sentence. Recognizing that the pronoun is the subject of the sentence, you should realize that *who* is needed. You can test your choice by substituting *he* for *who* and *him* for *whom*. (You can also substitute *she* or *they* for *who* and *her* or *them* for *whom* but we'll keep things simple.) Not only does substituting pronouns turn the question into a statement, but it clearly shows that *who* is the correct form.

He called last night. (correct)

Him called last night. (incorrect)

Now consider this example:

Who was there?

Whom was there?

Again, substitute *he* for *who* and *him* for *whom* and turn the questions into statements.

He was there. (correct)

Him was there. (incorrect)

At the risk of bringing back the horrors of taking the SATs, I want to go over this a couple more times just to make sure that you have this down. This next example uses the pronoun in a prepositional phrase. (For those of you who have been paying attention, this should be clue enough as to which form is required.)

To who did you send the package?

To whom did you send the package?

Test the pronouns by substituting *he* and *him*, and it becomes apparent which is the correct form.

You did send the package to he. (incorrect)

You did send the package to him. (correct)

But this was kind of a tricky example. Recognizing the prepositional phrase *to whom* is a clue that *whom* is correct, because an object of a prepositional phrase requires an objective case pronoun. The construction of the previous example, however, isn't as common as the one that follows:

Who did you send the package to?

At a first glance, most people would find this sentence to be just peachy keen. In fact, if this question were on the SATs, most people would only warrant a score worthy of a local community college. For in truth, the sentence is incorrect. In it, the prepositional phrase is split, the preposition *to* being placed at the end of the sentence (more on why you should never do this—at least on the SATs—in chapter 14). Although the construction is very common today in both informal and formal conversation and writing, it doesn't mean that you can use *who*. You still must use *whom* because an objective case pronoun is needed. Thus,

Whom did you send the package to?

When *who* or *whom* is used as a relative pronoun, its case is determined by the way it's used in the sentence. *Who* is still a subjective case pronoun, and *whom* is still an objective case pronoun. Being a part of a dependent clause, these pronouns aren't affected by any words outside the clause.

Here are some examples of a dependent clause introduced by *who* and *whom*. Which one do you think is correct? (Remember, your future depends on the right answer.)

The student who wins the essay contest will receive a cash prize.

The student whom wins the essay contest will receive a cash prize.

Got your thinking caps on? To determine the correct pronoun, first find the dependent clause, which is *who* or *whom wins the essay contest.* (Note that removing the clause leaves a complete sentence: *The student will receive a cash prize.*) Substitute *he* for who and *him* for *whom* in the dependent clause.

He wins the essay contest. (correct)

Him wins the essay contest. (Incorrect)

For those who got that right, you may proceed to an Ivy League school of your choice. For the others, well, I hear you can always get into Clown College. Here's another example to keep your brain cells a spinnin':

I'd love to meet the person who wrote this essay.

I'd love to meet the person whom wrote this essay.

In this sentence *who* or *whom wrote this essay* is the dependent clause. Substitute *he* for *who* and *him* for *whom* and you have the following:

He wrote this essay. (correct)

Him wrote this essay. (incorrect)

I feel it. You got that last one, didn't you? But for those who didn't, here's one last try:

I wonder who Bill contacted.

I wonder whom Bill contacted.

In this sentence *who* or *whom Bill contacted* is the clause. Substitute *he* for *who* and *him* for *whom* and you have:

Bill contacted he. (incorrect)

Bill contacted him. (correct)

Since *him* is correct, *whom* is the correct form.

If you didn't get that one either, don't be too hard on yourself. I said at the beginning of this section that this whole who/whom thing is confusing. But maybe you were okay with the transgender thing of the early '80s since things do have a way of evening themselves out in the end. Just be patient, and when in doubt, use *who*. Not that it'll be correct, but most people substitute *who* for *whom* and only the geniuses in grammar ever know the difference. Besides, you have a fifty-fifty chance of being right. Sure, people who use *who* and *whom* correctly are distinguished from the crowd, but they're often made fun of behind their backs. Like I said, things have a way of evening themselves out in the end.

Chapter 10

why can't they all just get along?

Now I'm going to dropkick you into one of the most difficult parts of the English language: irregular verbs. Of all the confusing topics in English grammar, few give people as much trouble as irregular verbs. Although the word *irregular* may be a great thing to see on a piece of furniture or an article of clothing, since it often translates into tremendous savings, it's a bad, bad word when dealing with verbs. That's because it means that just about anything goes and the verbs don't follow the standard patterns of form. Instead, they have evolved in their own maddening ways.

Irregular Verbs: The Misfits of English
Except for the verb *be*, which is the big enchilada of irregular verbs, all English verbs have five principal parts, or forms. The forms begin with the base, which is the form in present tense used with plural noun or pronoun subjects. The next form is the

present tense, third person singular. The third form is the past tense. The fourth form is the past participle, which requires the helping verbs *has*, *have*, or *had*. The final form is the present participle. A present participle has an –ing ending and requires a helping verb such as *am*, *is*, *was*, *are*, or *were*, depending on the subject. (For a refresher, return to chapter 1.)

Regular verbs, fortunately, make up the great majority of English verbs. They form their present, third person singular by adding an –s or –es, and form their past tense by added –d or -ed.

Here are three examples of regular verbs showing these five forms:

Base	Present (third person singular)	Past	Past Participle	Present Participle
bake	bakes	baked	(has, have, or had) baked	(am, is, was, are, or were) baking
finish	finishes	finished	(has, have, or had) finished	(am, is, was, are, or were) finishing
grin	grins	grinned	(has, have, or had) grinned	(am, is, was, are, or were) grinning

Yes, yes, for you sticklers out there, I realize that once in a while a final –*e* must be dropped when adding –*ing* to form the present participle (like with *bake* and *baking*), and yes, I know that some regular verbs, *grin* for example, require doubling a letter to form the past, past participle, and present participle forms (Man, you sure are observant!), but on the whole, these verbs are still considered regular.

Once you understand the five forms, there's nothing extraordinary about regular verbs. All regular verbs follow the same rules.

Unlike regular verbs, however, irregular verbs come with a few rules. They're the bad boys of the English language who do whatever they want and get all the hot girls. An irregular verb is a verb that doesn't follow the pattern of adding a _d_ or _ed_ to form its past or past participle forms. This can lead to huge confusion.

Following are some of the most common irregular verbs:

Base	Present Tense (third person singular)	Past Tense	Past Participle (has, have, had)	Present Participle (am, is, was, are, were)
bear	bears	bore	born, borne	bearing
beat	beats	beat	beaten	beating
become	becomes	became	become	becoming
begin	begins	began	begun	beginning
bite	bites	bit	bit, bitten	biting
blow	blows	blew	blown	blowing
break	breaks	broke	broken	breaking
bring	brings	brought	brought	bringing
build	builds	built	built	building
burn	burns	burned, burnt	burned, burnt	burning
burst	bursts	burst	burst	bursting
buy	buys	bought	bought	buying
catch	catches	caught	caught	catching
choose	chooses	chose	chosen	choosing
come	comes	came	come	coming
cost	costs	cost	cost	costing

Base	Present Tense (third person singular)	Past Tense	Past Participle (has, have, had)	Present Participle (am, is, was, are, were)
creep	creeps	crept	crept	creeping
cut	cuts	cut	cut	cutting
dig	digs	dug	dug	digging
dive	dives	dove, dived	dived	diving
do	does	did	done	doing
draw	draws	drew	drawn	drawing
drink	drinks	drank	drunk	drinking
drive	drives	drove	driven	driving
eat	eats	ate	eaten	eating
fall	falls	fell	fallen	falling
feel	feels	felt	felt	feeling
fight	fights	fought	fought	fighting
find	finds	found	found	finding
flee	flees	fled	fled	fleeing
fling	flings	flung	flung	flinging
fly	flies	flew	flown	flying
forget	forgets	forgot	forgotten, forgot	forgetting
freeze	freezes	froze	frozen	freezing
get	gets	got	gotten, got	getting
give	gives	gave	given	giving
go	goes	went	gone	going
grow	grows	grew	grown	growing
hang	hangs	hung,	hung, hanged	hanging
have	has	had	had	having
hear	hears	heard	heard	hearing
hide	hides	hid	hidden	hiding
hit	hits	hit	hit	hitting
hold	holds	held	held	holding

Base	Present Tense (third person singular)	Past Tense	Past Participle (has, have, had)	Present Participle (am, is, was, are, were)
hurt	hurts	hurt	hurt	hurting
keep	keeps	kept	kept	keeping
know	knows	knew	known	knowing
lay	lays	laid	laid	laying
lead	leads	led	led	leading
leave	leaves	left	left	leaving
lend	lends	lent	lent	lending
lie	lies	lay	lain	lying
lose	loses	lost	lost	losing
make	makes	made	made	making
mean	means	meant	meant	meaning
pay	pays	paid	paid	paying
prove	proves	proved	proved, proven	proving
read	reads	read	read	reading
ride	rides	rode	ridden	riding
ring	rings	rang	rung	ringing
rise	rises	rose	risen	rising
run	runs	ran	run	running
say	says	said	said	saying
see	sees	saw	seen	seeing
seek	seeks	sought	sought	seeking
send	sends	sent	sent	sending
set	sets	set	set	setting
shake	shakes	shook	shaken	shaking
shine	shines	shined, shone	shined, shone	shining
shoot	shoots	shot	shot	shooting
show	shows	showed	shown, showed	showing
shrink	shrinks	shrank	shrunk	shrinking

Base	Present Tense (third person singular)	Past Tense	Past Participle (has, have, had)	Present Participle (am, is, was, are, were)
sing	sings	sang	sung	singing
sink	sinks	sank	sunk	sinking
sit	sits	sat	sat	sitting
sleep	sleeps	slept	slept	sleeping
speak	speaks	spoke	spoken	speaking
spin	spins	spun	spun	spinning
steal	steals	stole	stolen	stealing
stand	stands	stood	stood	standing
stick	sticks	stuck	stuck	sticking
sting	stings	stung	stung	stinging
strike	strikes	struck	struck, stricken	striking
string	strings	strung	strung	stringing
strive	strives	strove	striven	striving
swear	swears	swore	sworn	swearing
swim	swims	swam	swum	swimming
swing	swings	swung	swung	swinging
take	takes	took	taken	taking
teach	teaches	taught	taught	teaching
tear	tears	tore	torn	tearing
think	thinks	thought	thought	thinking
throw	throws	threw	thrown	throwing
wake	wakes	woke, waked	woken, waked	waking
wear	wears	wore	worn	wearing
weave	weaves	wove	woven	weaving
win	wins	won	won	winning
wind	winds	wound	wound	winding
write	writes	wrote	written	writing

As you can see, these irregular verbs have no definable pattern, no guidelines, and no secret for revealing their key.

With irregular verbs, your best strategy is to learn them as you use them. Every time you use a form of an irregular verb correctly, you'll reinforce the correct form in your mind. If you aren't sure of one of the forms of an irregular verb, check a dictionary (although that assumes that you know how to spell it, and if not, you too may be a bad boy since oftentimes they lack higher education). Dictionaries always include the forms of irregular verbs after the base word.

Many people make mistakes with irregular verbs, and on that note, many women make mistakes with bad boys. The trick is to keep a dictionary close at hand, and your womanly instincts even closer.

Don't Get Tense about Verb Tenses

Sure, time is relative, but it's also a pain in the ass. We spend our days scurrying around like overwound wind-up toys so that we can do everything in the day that needs to get done. And when it comes to grammar, time is also a pain in the ass, and this ass pain is caused by verbs. Sure, verbs express action or state of being, but they also indicate time through their tense. Understanding the tenses of verbs is necessary for setting your thoughts within a clear time frame.

English verbs have six primary tenses:

- Present tense
- Past tense
- Future tense
- Present perfect tense

- Past perfect tense
- Future perfect tense

Each tense also has a progressive form that gives speakers and writers great latitude in expression. The following is a list of the tenses of English verbs, along with examples of classic performing artists throughout time.

- *Present tense* verbs show something that's happening right now, or indicate a current state of being. Note the examples.

  Elvis *gyrates* his hips.

  Billy Joel *is* a piano man.

- *Present progressive tense* is a form of the verb that expresses a continuing action, or an action that is in progress. Present progressive tense is formed by combining the helping verbs *am*, *is*, or *are* and the present participle of the main verb.

  Billy Holiday *is singing* the blues.

- *Past tense* verbs show action or state of being that has already happened.

  Sting *drove* his band to his country house.

  Frank Sinatra *was* a ladies man.

- *Past progressive tense* shows past action that continued over a period of time. It's formed by combining the helping verbs *was* or *were* with the present participle. Take a look and see:

  Britney *was cruising* to the stage when she realized that she forgot her talent.

- *Future tense* verbs indicate action or state of being that hasn't happened yet. Future tense verbs require *will* or *shall* with the present form.

  Elton *will fly* to England to buy some more whacky sunglasses.

  Louis Armstrong *will be* forever loved.

- *Future progressive tense* indicates action that will continue over a period of time in the future. It's formed by combining *will be* with the present participle, such as it is below.

  For Kelly Clarkson's tour, she *will be visiting* all the towns that wouldn't let her perform before she became an American Idol.

- *Present perfect tense* shows an action or state of being that started in the past and may still be going on in the present. It's formed by combining *have* or *has* with the past participle.

  I *have gone* to all of Tina Turner's concerts.

  Ozzy Osbourne *has been* difficult to understand for years.

- *Present perfect progressive tense* stresses past action that is continuing. It's formed by combining the helping verbs *have been* or *has been* with the present participle.

  Dolly Parton *has been living* with back pain her whole life, or at least she should be from carrying those two girls around all day.

- *Past perfect tense* indicates a past action or state of being that ended before another past action began. It is formed by combining the helping verb *had* with the past participle.

  Jack *had thought* that Black Eyed Peas were a kind of vegetable.

- *Past perfect progressive tense* is much like the past perfect tense, but it stresses continuing past action. It is formed by combining *had been* with the present participle.

David Hasselhoff *had been considering* various careers before he decided to try singing.

- *Future perfect tense* indicates a future action or state of being that will happen in the future before another future action. It is formed by combining *will have* or *shall have* with the past participle.

  Mariah Carey's concert *will have started* before we find our seats.

- *Future perfect progressive tense* is similar to future perfect tense, but it stresses the continuing action of a future event. It is formed by combining the helping verbs *will have been* with the present participle.

  By the end of this year, Cher *will have been singing* songs for what seems like three hundred years.

Time is a critical element for clear communication. Most ideas are expressed in a logical manner, generally according to time. Since time is expressed with verbs, understanding verb tenses is an important aspect for both speaking and writing with clarity. And understanding that a breast reduction may be the key to giving Dolly Parton some much-needed relief.

Taking Action on Active and Passive Constructions
Whom do you like better and respect more? People who sit back and passively let things happen to them, or the ones who take a clear, direct action? Most of us prefer the ones who take action, except of course for the sadomasochists who enjoy being blindfolded and stepped on by stiletto heels. We

know where people like this stand and their actions indicate their objectives.

Like active or passive people, verbs can be used in active or passive roles. Also known as active or passive voice, active and passive constructions may say the same thing but in quite different ways.

Here are some A&P examples on the S&M theme:

Passive	Active
The leather whip was removed by Lynda.	Lynda removed her leather whip.
Randy was excited by Jan's pole dance.	Jan's pole dance excited Randy.
The spike collar was played with by Steve.	Steve played with the spike collar.

After reading the examples, it should become obvious that active constructions are concise and clear, while passive constructions are wordy and weak. Effective speakers and writers rely on active constructions as much as they can to communicate clearly.

Here's another example:

The long, red nails were worn by Kim. (passive)
Kim wore the long red nails. (active)

In active constructions, the subject of the sentence performs the action. In passive constructions, the subject is acted upon. And in sadomasochism, either one can perform the action or be acted upon. In the previous passive example, *nails* is the subject of the sentence and it is acted upon (worn) by Kim. In the active construction, *Kim* is the subject of the sentence and she wore the nails.

Note that active constructions rely on the main verb, while passive constructions use a form of the verb *be* (in the example, *were*), combined with the past participle of the main verb. Using main verbs makes sentences stronger and more direct.

Although you should favor active constructions over passive ones in your speaking and writing, in some cases passive constructions will be a better choice because the passive construction will sound more natural. Consider this important yet non–S&M example:

A professional manages estate planning best. (active)

Estate planning is best managed by a professional. (passive)

In this example, the active construction sounds a bit awkward. The passive construction is smoother, and, perhaps even more importantly, places *estate planning* at the beginning of the sentence where it enjoys greater emphasis and focuses the reader's or listener's attention on the topic.

Overall, active constructions help listeners and readers to more easily understand what you're saying. In many cases, passive constructions, because of their wordiness and lack of energy, can muddle your expression. That's why you should strive to use active constructions in your speaking and writing, unless a passive construction presents your ideas more clearly. And if you are a sadomasochist, well, just beware of those stiletto heels. They really can leave quite a mark.

one last thing before you die of boredom

I know the name of this chapter sounds like an upbeat and happy topic, but the truth is . . . it is. (Fooled you, didn't I?) Well, at least the first section is. Not only are appositives a breeze to understand, but this section is relatively short. This fact thrills me, because writing about grammar takes a hell of a lot more time than simply reading it!

Being Positive about Appositives

An appositive is a noun or a pronoun that identifies or provides information about another noun or pronoun. An appositive phrase is made up of an appositive and its modifiers. Appositives and appositive phrases almost always follow the noun or pronoun they identify or explain, although, true, once in a while they may come before it. Appositive phrases are usually set off by commas.

In the following examples, the appositives are italicized. Also, the examples provide enlightening information about one of my favorite classic television shows of all time, *The Partridge Family*. Notice the use of commas, except for the first example where a comma is unnecessary because the appositive, *Chris*, is so closely related to the word it modifies, *uncle*, that it is almost a part of the word.

> My uncle *Chris* was the drummer in the band.
>
> Chris, *the drummer*, was replaced by another kid not long into the series.
>
> Lori Partridge, *the older sister*, could hear radio stations on her new braces.
>
> *The kid who only knew how to play the triangle,* Tracy, hardly had any lines on the show.
>
> They drove around on a school bus, *a multicolored vehicle*.
>
> Shirley, *the mom on the show*, must have taken a lot of Prozac to get through her day.

Was I right? Pretty easy stuff, huh? Ah, if only all of grammar was this easy to understand. As you can see, appositives are an efficient way to insert information that is helpful or necessary to fully understand a noun or pronoun. Used appropriately, appositives allow you to provide additional details while maintaining a smooth expression of your ideas. Unfortunately, we must now return from the era of classic television and back to reality where a more difficult part of grammar follows. So, put a smile on your face and c'mon get happy!

Those Mod and Happenin' Modifiers:
Adjectives, Adverbs, and Comparisons

As you remember from part 1 of the book, or from any Mad Libs game that you ever played as a kid, you know that adverbs (words like slowly, quickly, suddenly) modify verbs, adjectives, and other adverbs, and that adjectives (words like gooey, slimy, and stinky . . . those are the ones that always got a big laugh at Mad Libs) modify nouns and pronouns. For instance, in the sentence—The mod flower child twirled lazily in the sun—*mod* and *flower* are adjectives that describe the *child*, and *lazily* is an adverb that tells how she twirled. While it's true that nouns and verbs provide the meat of a sentence, it's the adjectives and the adverbs that give it the flavor. And if you're talking about flavor, no decade in history gave us as much flavor as the colorful 1960s, the decade that I'm devoting this segment to. So put on your tie-dye shirt and grow your hair long, because we're blastin' back to the past!

Believe it or not, even the turbulent '60s had grammar, so let's get back to figuring out those modifiers. In addition to using colorful adjectives and adverbs to modify words and provide hip detail to an otherwise dull sentence, you can also use them to make comparisons. Both adjectives and adverbs have a *positive* form, which is the base form of the word you'll find in the dictionary; a *comparative* form, in which two things are compared; and a *superlative* form, in which three or more things are compared. The comparative form for most adjectives and adverbs is created by adding —*er* to the base word, while the superlative form is created by adding —*est* to the base. Most adjectives and many adverbs of one and two syllables form their comparative and superlative forms in these manners. Yes, dude, I know this last paragraph may seem a bit hard to understand, and you probably had to read it a couple of times to understand it, but don't fret. I had to write it a few times to understand it as well. But as usual, here are some examples of adjectives that will make this totally turbulent concept a lot less turbulent, man.

Positive	Comparative	Superlative
old	older	oldest
young	younger	youngest
groovy	groovier	grooviest
cool	cooler	coolest
hip	hipper	hippest

Now here's an example using *big* that shows the three forms in action:

Laura has a *big* pimple on her nose. (positive)

Caryn has a *bigger* pimple on her nose. (comparative)

Mavis has the *biggest* pimple on her nose. (superlative)

See? Doesn't that make things all better? You've been using positive, comparative, and superlative adjectives your whole life and didn't even know it. Aren't you the gnarly one? It is worth noting that minor spelling changes can sometimes occur in the comparative and superlative forms. For example, the –*y* in *groovy* is changed to –*i* before adding –*er* or –*est*. With *hip*, the –*p* is doubled before adding the endings. But you being the gnarly one had probably picked out that minor detail.

❝ I'm a nervous flyer anyway, but when the captain announced that we were flying in the 'most best' conditions, I started to panic. If he can't master basic grammar, how the hell can he master an instrument panel?**❞**

—Vicki

For some adjectives of two syllables and most of three or more syllables, the words *more* or *most* are used with the base word to indicate the comparative and superlative forms. This avoids tongue-twisting constructions like the ones below:

Today's Hendrix concert is excitinger than last year's. (incorrect)

Today's Hendrix concert is the *excitingest* of all. (incorrect)

Today's Hendrix concert is *more exciting* than last year's. (correct)

Today's Hendrix concert is the *most exciting* of all. (correct)

So, Daddy-O, here are more examples of adjectives that use *more* and *most*:

Positive	Comparative	Superlative
attractive	more attractive	most attractive
excellent	more excellent	most excellent
colorful	more colorful	most colorful

Here are two more examples using adjectives correctly:

Sunflower is slicker than her sister Moon Unit, but Earth Lady is the *slickest* of the three chicks.

Brad is *more thrilling* than Bill, but Ben is the *most thrilling* of the three surfer dudes.

174 grammar sucks

Adverbs follow the same patterns for comparisons as adjectives. While most adverbs of one syllable form their comparative and superlative forms by adding *–er* and *–est* to their base words, most two-syllable adverbs, especially those ending in *–ly*, use *more* or *most* for their comparative and superlative forms. Consider the following examples of adverbs:

Positive	Comparative	Superlative
low	lower	lowest
fast	faster	fastest
high	higher	highest
smoothly	more smoothly	most smoothly

Here are some additional examples in which the adverbs *late*, *later*, and *latest* modify the verb *arrived*:

John arrived *late* for the protest.

Samantha arrived *later* than John.

Deanna arrived *latest* of all.

John shouted *furiously* in the protest line.

Samantha shouted *more furiously* than John in the protest line.

Deanna shouted *most furiously* of all in the protest line.

While most adjectives and adverbs follow the forms shown above, some are more antiestablishment and have irregular comparative and superlative forms. These hippie-like adjectives and adverbs are often misused. You should learn their forms, which follow:

Irregular Adjectives

Positive	Comparative	Superlative
good, well	better	best
bad, ill	worse	worst
many, much	more	most
little	littler, less	littlest, least

Irregular Adverbs

Positive	Comparative	Superlative
well	better	best
badly	worse	worst
much	more	most
far	farther, further	farthest, furthest

After taking a look at these forms for just a few moments, some potential problems become obvious. Several of the words can function as both adjectives and adverbs, depending upon their use and position in a sentence. But some forms can only function as either an adjective or an adverb, and this causes great confusion.

"My wife has this habit of telling everyone who leaves the house to 'drive careful.' I want to tell her that she should say 'drive carefully' instead, but she's so defensive that I know she'll tell me to 'drive careful' as she kicks me out of the house."

—Jeff

Let's start with *good*, *well*, *bad*, and *badly*. *Good* and *bad* are adjectives, *well* and *badly* are adverbs, but *well* can also be an adjective. Remember that adjectives modify nouns or pronouns. They can also follow linking verbs such as *be*, *feel*, *look*, *seem*, *appear*, *smell*, *sound*, and *taste*. Check out the examples:

> I caught a *good* wave this morning. (correct. *Good* is an adjective and modifies the noun *wave*.)
>
> Barb felt *bad* when she lost her roach clip. (correct. *Bad* is an adjective, follows the linking verb *felt*, and modifies *Barb*.)
>
> Having recovered from the hangover, Pete feels *well*. (correct. *Well* is an adjective, follows the linking verb *feel*, and modifies *Pete*.)

Note that *well* is typically used as an adjective to refer to health, appearance (for example, *well dressed*) or a satisfying condition (*all is well*). As an adverb, *well* is most often used to mean that something was done capably, as in these examples:

> Nick played *good* in his garage band. (incorrect. *Good* is an adjective and can't modify the verb *played*.)
>
> Nick played *well* in his garage band. (correct. *Well* is an adverb modifying the verb *played*.)

Let's take a peek at *bad* and *badly*. *Bad* is an adjective and *badly* is an adverb. Note the examples:

> After the love fest, everyone agreed that Jack had been a *bad* boy. (correct. *Bad* is an adjective and modifies *boy*.)
>
> Although it looked fresh, the alfalfa salad tasted *bad*. (correct. *Bad* is an adjective, follows the linking verb *tasted*, and modifies *salad*.)
>
> Cybil spoke *badly* of Kaelyn. (correct. *Badly* is an adverb and modifies the verb *spoke*.)

Marc's leg was *badly* broken after the sit-in. (correct. *Badly* is an adverb and modifies the verb phrase *was broken.*)

When making comparisons with the comparative and superlative forms, be sure to avoid double comparatives and double superlatives. Note the examples:

After my old man loosened up on my curfew hours, my partying was *more better* than ever. (incorrect)

After my old man loosened up on my curfew hours, my partying was *better* than ever. (correct)

The last wreck of my Deuce Coupe was the *most worst* of all the wrecks. (incorrect)

The last wreck of my Deuce Coupe was the *worst* of all the wrecks. (correct)

In cases where you wish to express the opposite degree of *more* or *most* with an adjective or adverb, use *less* or *least*. Note the examples:

To Mari, Elvis was *less important* than the Beatles.

Jerry was stoked to win the limbo contest but thought the medal was the *least significant* of all the others.

Adjectives and adverbs provide you with the opportunity to express your ideas in a broad range of degree and details. Using modifiers correctly can not only make your ideas vivid for your listeners and readers, but also enhance your stature as a person who understands language and grammar. On that note, we leave the subject of modifiers and the era of the turbulent sixties. So hang loose as we keep on truckin' down the road of grammar.

Part 3

how to become that annoying person who critiques others

Congratulations! You're now officially two-thirds finished with this book. If you were pregnant, you'd be starting your last trimester. Of course you'd also be suffering through gas, constipation, and hemorrhoids, so as hard as this grammar stuff is, it seems like a breeze by comparison.

Although you may be worried that you're entering the third and therefore most difficult part of the book, you may be surprised to find that it's not as hard as you imagined it to be. By now you're already familiar with things like clauses, phrases, and my stupid jokes, so there shouldn't be any big surprises. If anything, this last section of the book isn't so much to present new ideas, but rather to fine-tune your grammar skills and hone them as sharp as a thorn on a rose bush. I bet you thought I'd come up with a joke of some kind, but if you've ever been attacked by a nasty rose bush, you know just how sharp those mothers can be!

So take your time. Read slowly so that you can grasp every last detail and, of course, every bit of humor. Once you've completed this last section, you will have done what few before you have ever done, especially if you were one of the first people to buy this book.

Chapter 12

from santa and beyond: the different types of clauses

As we explained back in the olden days of part 1, clauses are groups of words that have both a subject and a predicate. There are also different kinds of clauses. An independent, or main, clause expresses a complete thought and can stand alone as a sentence (Remember? I called it a "wife"). A dependent, or subordinate, clause doesn't express a complete thought and can't stand alone (Remember? I called it a "husband"). Depending on their use in a sentence, dependent clauses can serve as nouns, adjectives, or adverbs.

Now, let's move on to some fresh material.

Adjective Clauses
When a dependent clause modifies a noun or a pronoun, it acts as an adjective and is therefore referred to as an adjective clause. Take a look:

The woman *who went on Weight Watchers* lost the greatest amount of weight. (The dependent clause modifies the noun *woman*.)

Adjective clauses, which are also known as *relative clauses*, are usually (but not always) introduced by relative pronouns: *who, whom, whose, which, what*, or *that*. They may also be introduced by a subordinating conjunction such as *when, why*, or *where*. (Compound relative pronouns such as *whoever, whomever, whichever*, and *whatever* may also begin adjective clauses.)

Here are some examples of adjective clauses and tempting tidbits to avoid when dieting:

Betty Crocker is the brand of frosting *that I like best.* (The clause modifies the noun *frosting*.)

Fatburger is the place *where you can get the best burgers.* (The clause modifies the noun *place*.)

The snack cakes, *whose makers are Dolly Madison and Hostess*, have the most irresistible creamy centers. (The clause modifies the noun *cakes*.)

Sometimes a relative pronoun that begins a dependent clause also serves as the subject of the clause it begins. Note the following in which *who* is the subject of the clause:

Colonel Sanders, *who created the secret blend of eleven herbs and spices*, is in part blamed for today's obesity problem.

In some cases, a relative pronoun may be the object of the clause it begins, or the object of a preposition in a clause. In the first example that follows, *whom* is the object of the clause, and in the second *whom* is the object of the preposition *to*.

The holiday fruitcake was offered to sweet-tooth Melanie, *whom everyone knows.*

Is Mrs. Fields the business woman *whom you look up to?*

In some sentences, *when* and *where* can introduce adjective clauses. Note the examples:

> Halloween is the time *when dentists everywhere do a little dance.* (The clause modifies the noun *time.*)
>
> I would love to visit Hershey, Pennsylvania, *where my favorite food is created.* (The clause modifies *Hershey, Pennsylvania.*)

In some adjective clauses, when the meaning of the clause is clear, a relative pronoun can be left out. Note the example in which the relative pronoun, *that,* can be left out without changing or confusing the meaning of the clause.

> This is the brand of cheesecake *that I devoured last night for dessert.*
>
> This is the brand of cheesecake *I devoured last night for dessert.*

Adverb Clauses

Unlike adjective clauses that modify nouns and pronouns, adverb clauses are used as adverbs and modify verbs, adjectives, and other adverbs. They have quite the inquisitive mind and generally answer the questions why? where? how? when? to what extent? or under what conditions?

Adverb clauses are introduced by subordinating conjunctions that join the clause with the rest of the sentence. Subordinating conjunctions not only introduce a dependent clause, but they also show the relationship between the dependent clause and the independent clause. For a list of subordinating conjunctions, see "Catchy Conjunctions" in chapter 1, page 23.

In the following examples the adverb clauses are italicized:

Christina jogs *because she wants to lose five pounds by the weekend.* (The clause modifies the verb *jogs* and answers the question *why*.)

As soon as they closed the "all you can eat" buffet, we left. (The clause modifies the verb *left* and answers the question *when*.)

Anna works less efficiently *than she did before she ate that can of Pringles.* (The clause modifies the adverb phrase *less efficiently* and answers the question *how*.)

Elliptical Clauses

Adverb clauses may be elliptical. In an *elliptical clause*, a word or words have been taken out; the reader or listener, however, understands the omitted words. In the following examples, the clauses are italicized and the omitted words are in parentheses:

While (she was) grocery shopping, Janice ate half a box of Ho Hos.

His brother is heavier *than Tom (is).*

Noun Clauses

Whereas an adjective or adverb clause is a modifier, a noun clause is actually a dependent clause that functions as a noun in a sentence. A noun clause has many faces and can work as the subject of an independent clause, a predicate nominative, a direct object, an indirect object, the object of a preposition, or an appositive.

Words that introduce noun clauses are many of the same words that can introduce adjective clauses (called relative pronouns) or adverb clauses (called subordinating conjunctions); when they introduce noun clauses, they're simply called introductory words. And you thought learning the names of the *Apprentice* finalists was hard!

Typical introductory words for noun clauses include the following:

- that
- which
- what
- whether
- whatever
- who
- when
- whoever
- where
- whomever

Following are some examples in which the noun clauses appear in italics:

What I require is more sprinkles on my ice cream cone. (The clause serves as the subject.)

Tessa's cream pie is *what I want for dessert.* (The clause serves as a predicate nominative.)

Bill told him *that he was hungry.* (The clause serves as a direct object.)

His belief, *that the diet pills are good for you,* is foolish. (The clause serves as an appositive.)

In some sentences, the introductory word of a noun clause can be left out without a loss of meaning:

Most people believe *(that) pot pies aren't really a dessert.*

At their most basic, clauses can stand alone as complete sentences, or they can be combined to form compound and complex sentences. But knowing that clauses may serve as complete sentences, or as adjectives, adverbs, or nouns, gives you a thorough understanding of sentence structure. Understanding how to lose weight and actually doing it is an even more difficult challenge, especially when there are people like Mrs. Fields, Colonel Sanders, and Betty Crocker weighing you down.

Avoiding Mistakes with Conjunctions, Relative Pronouns, and Clauses

While most of the words that introduce clauses are easy to use, some are the cause of many grammatical mistakes, especially the relative pronouns that introduce adjective clauses. Some of the most exasperating culprits are *than* and *then* (which is neither a relative pronoun nor a conjunction), *that* and *which*, and *who* and *whom* (which we've already covered). I suspect you're nodding your head in agreement, for you have probably had some trouble with these grammatical bad boys.

Then and Than

Than is a conjunction used for introducing the second part of a comparison. Avoid misusing it with *then*, which most commonly functions as an adverb. Note the examples of then/than and various other bad boys:

> The Fonz is older *then* his friend, Richie Cunningham. (incorrect)
>
> The Fonz is older *than* his friend, Richie Cunningham. (correct)
>
> James Dean will arrive *than*. (incorrect)
>
> James Dean will arrive *then*. (correct)
>
> First we'll go to dinner, and *than* we'll go to the Tommy Lee concert. (incorrect)

First we'll go to dinner, and *then* we'll go to the Tommy Lee concert. (**correct**)

That and Which

That and *which* are relative pronouns. Many people believe these two words are interchangeable and can be used in place of each other. They can—but only sometimes. *That* is used only with restrictive clauses (a clause that is essential to the meaning of the sentence and that I'll talk more about a little later). Moreover, *that* is used to refer to either persons or things. *Which* can be used with either restrictive or nonrestrictive clauses (a clause that isn't essential to the meaning of a sentence and that I'll also talk more about later), but it should be used to refer only to things. Note the examples:

The report about Kevin Federline *that everyone found so upsetting* was based on faulty data. (This is a restrictive clause, which is essential to the meaning of the sentence.)

The group *that was permitted to enter the Jude Law movie premier early* got the best seats. (This is a restrictive clause, which is essential to the meaning of the sentence.)

The stack of magazines, *which happened to contain nude photos of Colin Farrell*, was delivered to the wrong building. (This is a nonrestrictive clause, which is not essential to the meaning of the sentence.)

Most subordinating conjunctions and relative pronouns present few problems with usage when introducing dependent clauses. But there are some that account for most of the mistakes people make with these words. These are definitely the bad boys of grammar and, unless you understand them, you should avoid them at all costs.

As we discussed in part 1, a comma lets your reader know when he needs to take a pause, which helps bring clear meaning to your words. In writing, you must include all different types of punctuation to indicate the pauses (generally commas, semicolons, and colons) and stops (periods, question marks, and exclamation points). But punctuation is particularly important when you're dealing with clauses—let's examine why

Comma Mia!

There are all kinds of things that people disagree on. Some people think that being a Democrat is better than being a Republican. Some people think that the city is a better place to live than the country. And of course, some people think that anchovies make a tasty pizza topping while others feel they make them sick. Commas are another topic that people disagree about. Some writers like to sprinkle in so many commas that the reader feels like he's in literary stop-and-go traffic. Others use them so sparingly that their work feels like one giant run-on sentence. Putting different writing styles aside, there are several rules of the comma road that must be strictly followed when you're dealing with clauses in order to be grammatically correct. So I'd like to take a few moments, and a few paragraphs, to fill you in on what they are.

Correct comma usage is vital when dealing with clauses, as clauses have a subject and predicate and can either be independent and able to stand alone, or be dependent and need to be combined with an independent clause. When you understand how to punctuate clauses, only then can you consider yourself a master of commas. In other words, a comma sutra!

Introductory Adverb Clauses

While we're on the subject of comma sutra, let's dedicate the examples in this particular section to everyone's favorite subject: sex. Let's start with the *introductory adverb clause.* The introductory adverb clause needs to be set off from the rest of the sentence with a comma. The "introductory" of sex, however, should be set off with foreplay. Note the following examples, in which the adverb clauses, and sometimes the method of foreplay, are italicized:

> *If you're a really good kisser,* call me.
>
> *After the sports recap was aired,* he resumed giving her a back rub.
>
> *When you finish the massage oil,* you can find more in the end table.

Since adverb clauses, like adverbs, can be placed in different parts of a sentence, introductory clauses can often be rewritten and positioned after the main clause without changing the meaning of the sentence. Of course, then they're no longer an introductory clause. In such cases, a comma isn't needed, unless the construction of the sentence makes the meaning confusing or vague. Note the previous examples, now with the adverb clauses following the main clauses and without commas to set them off from the rest of the sentence:

> Call me *if you're a really good kisser.*
>
> He resumed giving her a back rub *after the sports recap was aired.*
>
> You can find more in the end table *when you finish the massage oil.*

A word to the wise: When you're rewriting sentences such as in the examples above, they sometimes may become muddled. When you put an adverb clause, which could serve as an introductory clause, after a main clause, there can be small distortions in time and logic. In the second example, for instance, since the sports recap came first in actual time, it may make more sense to set the clause containing the recap as an introductory clause. Similarly, in the third example, the person to whom the sentence is addressed must run out of massage oil before he goes to find more of it in the end table. Therefore, it would seem to make more sense to use the adverb clause as an introductory clause. I don't mean to nitpick. These are small points, but the person who has hopes of being a true comma sutra needs to pay attention to these minor points (and foreplay. You can never pay too much attention to foreplay).

Restrictive vs. Nonrestrictive Clauses

Along with functioning as adverbs, adjectives, or nouns, dependent clauses may be either restrictive or nonrestrictive. The distinction between the two depends on whether commas are needed to set off the clause from the rest of the sentence.

A *restrictive clause*, also known as an *essential clause*, is necessary to the meaning of a sentence. Restrictive clauses can't be taken out of a sentence without clouding or changing its meaning. Because they're necessary to the meaning of the sentence, restrictive clauses are not set off with commas. To prove my point, here's an example of just what all this gibberish translates into when it becomes an actual sentence:

Almost every man *who tried to skip the kissing part of lovemaking* failed to satisfy his partner.

If the clause is removed from the sentence, the sentence becomes *Almost every man failed to satisfy his partner*, which is obviously not the writer's intent, nor his partner's. As you can clearly see, the clause is essential for the sentence to have the meaning that it was meant to have.

Here's another example of a restrictive clause:

He saw an adult video *that supplied the inspiration for their evening together.*

If the clause is removed, the sentence becomes *He saw an adult video*. On its own, this doesn't convey the writer's original meaning. The clause is the important element of the sentence, just as the video was the important element in their evening. Without it, this is just a sentence about an ordinary guy watching a porno movie, like all ordinary guys do.

Unlike restrictive clauses, which are necessary to the meaning of a sentence, *nonrestrictive* clauses aren't necessary at all. The only thing that nonrestrictive clauses do is provide more information about something, or explain it, but they can be left out of a sentence without changing its meaning or intent. A nonrestrictive clause does, however, give the sentence a little something-something. It's a grammatical leather whip or a red garter belt. It certainly gives something extra, but it's not mandatory in the sentence, nor for that matter is the whip or the garter. But in either case, it sure doesn't hurt!

Because they're not crucial to the meaning of a sentence, nonrestrictive clauses should be set off from the rest of the sentence with commas. Here's an example of how it would look:

Canned whipped cream, *which even comes in flavors like chocolate and French vanilla*, opens up a world of possibilities.

Although the clause provides an interesting tidbit of information to the sentence, it's not essential to its basic meaning, which is that whipped cream opens up a world of possibilities. Granted, it may be crucial information if you're looking for a tasty whipped topping for your homemade silk pie, but it's not all that relevant in the sentence above. It may interest you to know that just about all clauses that modify proper nouns are nonrestrictive, as this next example shows.

Gracie Peterson, *who lives down the street*, prefers the French vanilla flavor.

That Gracie lives down the street is not essential to the intent of the sentence, but it is a helpful bit of information for whoever will be bringing her the vanilla whipped topping.

And here's one more example:

The blindfold, *which was made from the finest quality silk*, made for some interesting role playing.

In this sentence, the clause provides additional information about the quality of the blindfold, but it certainly isn't important to the meaning of the sentence. What is important is that you should go out and get yourself a blindfold if you want to do some role-playing yourself.

The rules for using commas with restrictive and nonrestrictive clauses seem simple enough: Restrictive clauses, which are necessary to the meaning of a sentence, shouldn't be set off with commas; nonrestrictive clauses, which aren't necessary to the meaning of a sentence, require commas to set them off from the rest of the sentence. And here's a little more. The relative pronoun *that* is only used with restrictive clauses, but the relative pronoun *which* can be used with either restrictive or nonrestrictive clauses. When referring to people, use the relative pronouns *who*, *whose*, and *whom*. Unfortunately, it's not quite so easy to recognize these things all the time. Some clauses, depending on a subtle shift in emphasis or intent, may be restrictive or nonrestrictive. They're the hermaphrodite of the English language. Note the use of the commas, or the absence of the commas, in the following examples:

Men, *who tire after having sex*, will roll over and play "beached whale."
Men *who tire after having sex* will roll over and play "beached whale."

The first sentence contains a nonrestrictive clause, but the second, which is almost the same sentence, contains a restrictive clause. If you think about the two sentences carefully, you'll notice a subtle shift in meaning. The first sentence implies that all men will roll over and play "beached whale." The clause provides information that supports this implication, but the clause is not necessary. In the second sentence, however, the restrictive clause alters the meaning of the sentence by implying that only those men who tire after having sex will roll over and play "beached whale." Granted, I know that the second sentence doesn't make any sense anyway because all men play "beached whale" after having sex, but you get my point. The inclusion of the commas changes the clause from restrictive to nonrestrictive, which therefore changes the meaning of the sentence.

The author of those words needs to know the difference between restrictive and nonrestrictive clauses, or he may write something that he doesn't mean. Speakers also need to be aware of the differences as well. A speaker who pauses at the beginning and ending of a clause in his or her normal, everyday conversation sends a message that the clause is nonrestrictive and not necessary to the meaning of the sentence. This can be a big no-no if in fact the clause is actually restrictive.

Knowing grammar and using it with precision gives you a significant advantage when you share your ideas through your speaking or your writing. As you master more and more of the fine points of grammar, you should incorporate your new knowledge into your overall communication skills. And being the true comma sutra that you are, you should also include your new knowledge about that chocolate whipped cream. It's a real crowd pleaser!

Chapter 13

the study of phraseology

Everyone in the "grammar know" understands that the most important groups of words in sentences are clauses, which contain the ever so popular nouns and verbs. But right behind this "A" list of word groups is the "B" list—the phrases. Sure, phrases can't get in at all the hot new, trendy restaurants, nor will they be seated in the front row of any awards show, but nonetheless, they still do enjoy some degree of box office success.

As I hope you remember from the first two parts of the book, a phrase is a group of words that supplies important details to a subject, a verb, an object, or a complement. If clauses and their nouns and verbs give sentences their basic form, it's phrases that expand these sentences and provide them with the details that they so desperately need to make them interesting. But don't expand them too much, since a leading lady can turn into a character actress in less time than you can say "Dunkin' Donuts."

The Fine Points about Phrases

There are many different kinds of phrases that are used by both the Hollywood elite and the up-and-coming ingénues in both writing and speaking. These phrases include the prepositional phrase, the appositive phrase, the absolute phrase, and the verbal phrase, which can be divided into the infinitive phrase, the gerund phrase, and the participial phrase. Since we've already covered prepositional phrases ("Party on Prepositional Phrases," page 41) and appositive phrases ("Being Positive about Appositives," page 169), let's focus our attention in this section on the other kinds of phrases. As you can see by the many paragraphs that follow, there is quite a lot to say about them.

Absolute Phrases

First up, is the loveable *absolute phrase*. No, this is not a trendy new vodka drink; it's just another cast member in our production of phrases. An absolute phrase stands out from the others by containing both a subject and an adjective phrase, which in most cases is a participial phrase. In general, an absolute phrase adds related material to a sentence and modifies entire clauses or sentences. Here are a couple of examples of its work for your review, with the absolute phrases in italics:

> The old Hollywood neighborhood, *its once stately homes crumbling with age*, brought tears to my eyes.
>
> *The glow of the morning sun brightening the eastern sky,* Sasha waited for her scene to begin.

Verbal Phrases

Next comes the *verbal*. A verbal is a word formed from a verb and can play many different roles in a sentence, for example, a noun, an adjective, or that ever-elusive adverb. Verbals come in three different forms: infinitives, gerunds, and participles. When a verbal is combined with other words, each of these three forms then becomes a phrase—an infinitive phrase, a gerund phrase, or a participial phrase. Let's analyze each of these phrases separately, because if we did it all at the same time, it'd be rather confusing.

Infinitives

An *infinitive* is made up of a verb plus the word *to*. Some examples of an infinitive are *to laugh*, *to smile*, *to run*, and so on. An infinitive phrase is made up of an infinitive and its modifiers, subject, or objects. The multitalented infinitive phrase can play many roles, such as a noun, an adjective, or even a temperamental adverb in a sentence. As nouns, they can be subjects, predicate nominatives, or even objects. Here are some examples of just the kind of work an infinitive phrase is capable of. The infinitive phrases are italicized in each sentence:

> *To fail the screen test* was not an option. (The infinitive phrase serves as a subject.)
>
> His goal after winning the Emmy was *to be a millionaire*. (The infinitive phrase serves as a predicate nominative.)
>
> Bryan plans *to start a business*. (The infinitive phrase serves as a direct object.)
>
> The spa vacation gave the actress a chance *to relax a little* after her hard role as Girl #2. (The infinitive phrase serves as an adjective modifying *chance*.)
>
> Rhonda waited *to begin her scene*. (The infinitive phrase serves as an adverb modifying *waited*.)

Gerunds

The next star in this production is a *gerund*. A gerund is a form of a verb that can also be used as a noun (remember the *–ing* ending?). A gerund is like a character actor that can play many different parts. In this case a gerund can star as a subject, an object, or a predicate nominative in a sentence. For more information on gerunds that are used as subjects, see "Super Gerunds: Our Superheroes of Irregular Subjects and Phrases" on page 96. To get an up-close and personal look at a gerund, you can either hang out at Rodeo Drive in Beverly Hills, or you can just check out the following sentences below:

> *Winning an Oscar* is half of Hollywood's goal in life. (The gerund phrase functions as the subject.)
>
> Bob dislikes *working with this director*. (The gerund phrase serves as the direct object.)
>
> Joanie is *running with a bad agent*. (The gerund phrase serves as a predicate nominative.)

Participles

Now let's move on to something new: *participles*. A *participle* is a form of a verb that can play the demanding role of an adjective. Present participles end in *–ing* and show that the action is currently taking place. Past participles of regular verbs always end in *–ed* or *–d* and show that the action has already occurred. The past participles of irregular verbs may vary, but usually end in *–en*, *–n*, or *–t*. Here are some examples of these very diverse and temperamental present and past participles of the verbs:

Present	Past	Past Participle	Present Participle
walk	walked	walked	walking
begin	began	begun	beginning
fall	fell	fallen	falling

To see more of the various works of these regular and irregular verbs, as well as their many forms, see "Very Vexing Verbs" on page 10 and "The Irregular Verbs: Misfits of English" on page 157.

Next up is the ever so popular *participial phrase*. A participial phrase consists of a present or a past participle that's paired up with modifiers, objects, or complements. The participle usually introduces the phrase, and the complete phrase functions as an adjective to modify a noun or pronoun. Here are some examples in which the star of the show, the participial phrase, is italicized so it will look wonderful for its red-carpet moment:

> *Having decided to become a movie star*, Sheri bought a plane ticket for Hollywood. (The phrase modifies *Sheri*.)
>
> The crowd, *increasing rapidly*, almost covered the red carpet at the movie premier. (The phrase modifies *crowd*.)
>
> *Surprised by the hint of cilantro*, the celebrity yelled at Wolfgang Puck for the horrible pizza. (The phrase modifies *celebrity*.)

Understanding the different types of phrases and the many ways that they can add details to a sentence will allow you to express yourself more clearly and efficiently. Having these star-studded phrases by your side can make your words stand out from the words of others, as well as get you that all important center table at Spago. Just remember to look your best or else you run the risk of being photographed as a "Grammar Don't."

Mr. Beau-Dangling Modifier

Cute pun aside, a dangling modifier is quite a serious matter, grammatically speaking, that is. As you can imagine, it's not a good idea to have anything dangle, as it may easily be lost or cut off—and phrases are no exception to this rule. In general, phrases are best placed as close as possible to the words they are supposed to modify. If they aren't, there needs to be a strong link between the phrase and the word to which it relates. If this doesn't happen, the meaning of the sentence can become lost in the shuffle. It may not be clear what word a phrase is supposed to modify, or maybe the phrase has no word to modify at all. When a phrase doesn't modify a word in a sentence, the phrase just hangs there. It's like a booger on the nose of pretty woman, who, for the first time in years, is on a date with a guy that she really, really likes. Sorry for the gross analogy, it's just one of those ugly memories that comes back to haunt me from time to time. Believe me, I have plenty of other dating memories that you'll see from the examples in this section.

Not all types of phrases are guilty of dangling. In fact, only certain types of phrases are especially vulnerable. Participial phrases are a perfect example because they function as adjectives but they arise from a verb. Being that they're a kind of hybrid, like a Prius, or even a mule, speakers and writers sometimes rely on them just as they would rely on verbs. After all, participial phrases describe action. Here's an example of a participial phrase in action right now:

> *Jumping out of the way,* my blind date avoided my line of sight so that he could easily slip out the door and officially stand me up.

This phrase clearly shows action, as well as complete humiliation on my part. But it also modifies my blind date by describing him as *jumping out of the way*, and as an insensitive buffoon.

In their excitement to use the action that's supplied by a participial phrase, people sometimes will include the phrase itself but forget to put in the word that it should be modifying. When this happens, the result can be a dangling participial phrase, or, as it's commonly referred to, a dangling modifier. A dangling modifier—which might be another type of phrase as well, provided that it doesn't have a word to modify—just hangs on in the sentence with nothing to anchor it. It's lost in a sea of despair, feeling all alone in the world, with no one to hold it at night or send it flowers on its birthday (sorry, there I go remembering again). You might think of a dangling modifier as the loneliest phrase in the English language.

Consider the following example:

> *Rewinding the answering machine*, it was clear that no one had left a phone message for an entire month.

The phrase is dangling because it doesn't modify any specific word. Who was rewinding the answering machine?

Here are more examples, but this time, the corrections are included as well:

> *Waiting alone for a table*, the restaurant was packed with couples. (dangling modifier—Was *the restaurant* waiting for a table?)
>
> *Waiting alone for a table*, I realized that the restaurant was packed with couples. (correct; the subject is *I*)
>
> *Watching TV for the fifth Saturday night in a row*, the flash of lightning and sudden thunder outside startled me. (dangling modifier—Were the lightning and thunder watching TV?)
>
> *Watching TV for the fifth Saturday night in a row*, I was startled by the flash of lightning and sudden thunder outside. (correct; the subject is *I*)

Walking down the aisle with all the Valentine's Day candy, the heart-shaped boxes made me want to cry. (dangling modifier—Were the heart-shaped boxes walking down the aisle with the Valentine's Day candy?)

Walking down the aisle with all the Valentine's Day candy, I wanted to cry because of the heart-shaped boxes. (correct; the subject is *I*)

As you can see from the examples, my life is one big pathetic ball of loneliness and despair. You can also see that dangling phrases can usually be fixed. The fix usually only requires a little tweaking or rethinking, but the small effort pays back huge dividends. Ah, if only a person's love life were so easily repaired!

Misplaced Modifiers

Don't you just hate it when you misplace things? I for one can never find my car keys. It always seems that they've found a better hiding place than Bin Laden. Another thing I have a habit of misplacing is my modifiers. But unlike the missing car keys that cause me so much frustration, a misplaced modifier causes frustration to the reader. That's because the reader, or listener if I'm speaking, has to put forth a lot more time and effort in understanding just what the heck I'm trying to say. And as you know, no one likes putting forth a lot of effort to do anything.

A misplaced modifier is actually quite similar to a dangling modifier, but whereas a dangling modifier is lost in a sentence without having any word to modify, a misplaced modifier modifies a word other than the one that it's supposed to. Therefore, like those damn car keys, the modifier is misplaced. In most cases, a misplaced modifier can be fixed by simply changing around the wording of the sentence or rewriting a few words. The lost car keys, on the other hand, can only be fixed by an exhaustive room-by-room search and the inevitable call to the locksmith.

Here are some examples of misplaced modifiers along with their corrections. As you've learned by now, Grasshopper, the misplaced modifiers will be in italics:

I finally found my sunglasses *looking out of my back window.* (The misplaced modifier makes it seem that the sunglasses were looking out the window.)

Looking out of my back window, I finally found my sunglasses. (correct)

Showing his bright feathers, Eddie photographed the peacock. (The misplaced modifier makes it seem that Eddie was showing his bright feathers. Sure, this might make the reader giggle at your description of Eddie, but there's an equal chance that the reader might also be giggling at your weak grasp of grammar.)

Eddie photographed the peacock *showing his bright feathers.* (correct)

Stretching high into the sky, Gabriela reached the jagged peaks. (The misplaced modifier makes it sound like Gabriela should pursue a career on a women's basketball team. But once the sentence is corrected, it's clear that all she did was look at some really tall peaks.)

Gabriela reached the jagged peaks, *stretching high into the sky.*

Getting someone's attention when you write is hard enough work on its own without making your reader struggle to make sense of your material. If they have to work at understanding what you're trying to convey, chances are that they'll simply become tired of reading your material. Unless, of course, your mistakes make them laugh, since misplaced modifiers tend to bring out a chuckle or two. If this happens, they're sure to remember what you wrote, but not for the right reasons.

In sum, make certain that you place your modifiers as close to the words that they're supposed to modify as possible so that the relationship between the two is clear. And while I'm doling out advice, make sure that you put your car keys in a predesignated spot every time you come home, a spot that's as close to your front door as possible. Believe me, both of these simple tricks will save you a lot of frustration down the road.

Chapter 14

these are a few of my least favorite things

We've all been warned about the dangers of splitting an infinitive. But how many of us really know what a split infinitive is? Not many, I guess. So let me take this opportunity to reveal the secret behind this well-known, albeit not well-understood, grammatical danger.

Don't Split Hairs about Split Infinitives

As you've already learned, an infinitive is a form of a verb that follows the word *to*. Although the word *to* usually starts off a prepositional phrase, it can also take on a special role in an infinitive. An infinitive may be used as a subject of a sentence, a predicate nominative, a direct object, or an adjective or adverb. An infinitive phrase is made up of an infinitive, its modifiers, complements, and, of course, a subject.

The following are some examples of infinitives as well as
infinitive phrases. Note that the infinitives are—say it with
me—italicized.

> The way *to succeed* is *to persevere*. (infinitives)
>
> *To give* is better than *to receive*. (infinitives)
>
> Gianna's favorite pastime is *to shop at flea markets*. (infinitive phrase)

Now that you're clear on what an infinitive is (and if
you're not, you can reread the above paragraph and examples; we'll wait for you), you need to know how *not* to cause
it to split. I guarantee that every one of you has split an
infinitive at some point in your lives, and you weren't even
aware that you committed this heinous sin. But those days
are over, for from here on out, you're going to know how to
take precautions to prevent this peril from ever occurring
again (drum roll please). A split infinitive happens when the
two parts of an infinitive are separated by another word or
words. There. That's it. It's that simple.

Here are a couple of examples to make this even clearer:

> Tired of being berated on the job, Matt decided simply *to tell* his boss
> that he was quitting. (infinitive)
>
> Tired of being berated on the job, Matt decided *to simply tell* his boss
> that he was quitting. (split infinitive)

See the difference? One says *to tell*, which keeps the infinitive packed tightly together, and the other puts the word
simply in between them so that they're split apart. You may
be asking yourself, "What's the big deal anyway? What's
so horrific about splitting an infinitive? It's not like there's
been a natural disaster or that they've stopped making Double Stuf Oreos."

In some ways, you're right. It wasn't so long ago that split infinitives were considered to be examples of faulty grammar. Even today, some experts, particularly grammar purists, still pooh-pooh a sentence when it has a split infinitive in it. But like most things in life, like segregation laws and how many blades they pack into a razor, things have a tendency to change. These days there is a whole new relaxed attitude on splitting an infinitive, and it's not looked upon as the sin it once was.

Problems of using split infinitives can arise when a speaker or writer puts a long or complicated split infinitive into what would otherwise be a clear expression. Then all bets are off and it's never a wise thing to do. Here are some examples of confusing split infinitives:

> Stan had *to repeatedly tell* her of his love for her.
>
> Stan had *to over and over again tell* her of his love for her.
>
> The little boy tried *to quietly tiptoe* to the kitchen and snatch a cookie.
>
> The little boy tried *to quietly and quickly tiptoe* to the kitchen and snatch a cookie.

These examples show the good and the bad of the split infinitive. In the first example, *to tell* is split apart by the

66 "My Aunt Rhoda was an English teacher and she always reprimands me whenever I split an infinitive. You'd think it would make me stop doing it by now, but all it's done is make me not want to sit next to her at Thanksgiving." 99

—Lisa

word *repeatedly*. This doesn't really undermine or muddle the meaning of the sentence, and most people would find it to be an acceptable construction. But in the second example the words *over and over again* split the infinitive up past the point of being acceptable. Unlike in the first example, this results in a wordy construction that drains the sentence, and often the listener or reader, of energy. The same thing happens with the third and fourth sentences. *To quietly tiptoe* is an acceptable split infinitive, at least for most people, because they won't have a problem following along. But when it suddenly becomes *to quietly and quickly tiptoe*, the sentence becomes more like a *War and Peace* novel and edges toward wordiness.

The second examples of each pair show the true and shocking horror of what can happen when an infinitive is split in the truest sense. In fact, even the most relaxed grammar purist would agree that those last two ugly sentences should be surrounded by yellow CAUTION police tape and treated as a grammar crime scene. For they're examples of awkward construction in the truest sense.

Now that I've shown you the full range of emotions that are caused from splitting an infinitive, from the casual, nonchalant attitude to the shocking potential for confusion, I have one more point to reveal. For believe it or not, in some instances, splitting an infinitive may actually work better than not splitting it at all. Here's an example of what I mean:

David resolved *to courageously confront* his enemy.

See? This is a definite case of a split infinitive. The infinitive *to confront* has been split by the word *courageously*. But in this instance, the action of splitting it actually helps the sentence and makes it more descriptive. It becomes smoother, clearer, and more direct. It could, of course, be rewritten in a variety of ways:

> David resolved to confront his enemy courageously.
>
> Courageously David resolved to confront his enemy.
>
> David, courageously, resolved to confront his enemy.

In each of these examples, however, some of the vigor of the first sentence is lost. Thus, in many instances, whether or not to split an infinitive comes down to a question of style and practicality. If splitting an infinitive enhances a sentence, the infinitive should no doubt be split. On the other hand, if splitting an infinitive undermines the clarity or flow of the sentence, it should definitely not be split. Just bear in mind that split infinitives should never be long or complex and should only strengthen the sentence rather than weaken it. Is that clear? Probably not. In fact, you were probably less confused before, when all you knew about split infinitives was that you shouldn't use them but had no idea what a split infinitive actually was.

Moody Verbs

We can all get moody from time to time. We get mad when we're in a rush and hit bumper-to-bumper traffic. We get sad when we discover that we accidentally recorded *Full House* instead of *House*. And of course, we get elated when we finally, for the first time in our life, choose the fastest line at the grocery store checkout. As it turns out, we humans are not the only things that can get moody. Believe it or not, verbs can get moody as well.

Along with showing action or indicating a state of being, verbs can be categorized according to three different moods: the indicative, the imperative, and the subjunctive. True, these moods are a bit more confusing than your average "dwarflike" mood of happy or grumpy or dopey, but it's a mood nonetheless. A verb's mood shows the speaker's or writer's attitude in regard to his or her words. For example, you can express a fact, an opinion, a hypothetical condition, a wish, or a command by the way something is said or written, or, in other words, its mood can affect its meaning.

Indicative Mood

The first mood we'll discuss is the *indicative mood*. Sentences in the indicative mood can make an assertion, state facts, offer an opinion, or even ask a question. By far, most of the verbs that you use in ordinary speaking and writing will be in the indicative mood.

The following examples highlight verbs that are feeling rather indicative:

> Snow White departs at noon.
>
> The evil queen gave piano lessons for several years.
>
> I think that Prince Charming is a top-notch skier.
>
> Do you want an apple for dessert?

Imperative Mood

The next mood is called the *imperative mood*. It's used to express direct commands, to make requests, or to provide instructions. Here are a few examples:

> Go to the castle and make a left at the toadstool.

Please pass the soap.

Put the woodland creatures in the backyard.

The indicative and imperative moods of verbs present very few problems for most people, unless of course that person is so enraged from their confusion with grammar that they can't concentrate. If that's the case, then relax in a nice hot bath with a cold martini.

Subjunctive

For the rest of you who are following along, let's lift your mood by continuing on to the next verb mood: the *subjunctive*. Unlike the tranquil indicative and imperative moods that are quite simple and straightforward, the subjunctive mood is a rather tricky one. In fact, it can be a huge source of trouble, even for those few people in the world who otherwise have a relatively good understanding of grammar.

The subjunctive mood is all about expressing an uncertainty. It's used to express wishes, declare hypothetical conditions, and issue indirect commands or requests. You can usually recognize the subjunctive mood pretty easily since it often appears in clauses that begin with *if*, *that*, or *as though*, or includes words such as *request*, *insist*, *urge*, and *recommend*. Here are a few examples of this uncertain mood of the subjunctive verb:

Doc asked that Dopey *manage* the mines. (a request)

Sleepy insisted that Snow White *finish* her song. (an indirect command)

The hunter recommended that the queen *discuss* the problem with the magic mirror. (a hypothetical condition)

If Dopey and Snow White *were* here, I'd ask for their autographs. (a wish)

See? What did I tell you? It's very confusing, even in these lighthearted, fairy-tale sentences. Hey, I'm writing about this stuff and even I still find it really, really hard to understand at times. In fact, it makes me angry and frustrated and in desperate need of chocolate. But if the subjunctive mood isn't confusing enough, let's move on to something that's almost guaranteed to put you in a foul mood: the different tenses of these three different moods. Hold on to your hats, everyone, because this is going to be a bumpy ride!

Tense Moods

For most verbs, the only difference in the present tense between the indicative and subjunctive moods appears in the forms that are used with a singular noun or the pronouns he, she, or it. In the present tense subjunctive, singular nouns and these same pronouns (he, she or it) use the base form of the verb. Do you still have your hat on? I told you there'd be bumps. Here are a few examples of verbs that are in the present tense in hopes of clarifying this complicated matter even more:

Indicative Mood

I walk	you walk	he walks	she walks	it walks	Elaine walks
I leave	you leave	he leaves	she leaves	it leaves	Joe leaves
I am	you are	he is	she is	it is	Paula is

Subjunctive Mood

I walk	you walk	he walk	she walk	it walk	Elaine walk
I leave	you leave	he leave	she leave	it leave	Joe leave
I be	you be	he be	she be	it be	Paula be

(Notice that the pronoun *I* needs the base form of verbs in both the indicative and subjunctive moods, except for the verb *be*. Also notice that it looks like I made a typo when I wrote *he walk, she walk, it walk,* and *Elaine walk,* but I didn't.)

Let's go over all this one more time before we move on. If you read it again, it just may sink in. In the present tense for most verbs, there is only one difference between the indicative and subjunctive. The difference is used with singular nouns, or the pronouns *he, she,* or *it.* In the present subjunctive, these all use the base form of the verb. The base form of the verb is the form that appears in the dictionary. There, I hope that helped.

To put this into context even more, let's consider the third-person indicative and subjunctive forms in the present tense. Here are some examples, with the subjunctives being italicized:

> Snow White walks with the friendly deer every night for exercise. (indicative)
>
> Dopey suggested to Happy that he *walk* with Snow White as well. (subjunctive)
>
> All seven dwarves leave the mines for home at 6 p.m. every evening. (indicative)
>
> Snow White requested that Sneezy *leave* work early today. (subjunctive)

Although the verb *be* has three forms in the indicative present tense (*am, is,* and *are*), its base form is required in the present tense of the subjunctive for both singular and plural. Consider the examples:

Indicative

| I am | you are | he, she, it is | we are | they are |

Subjunctive

| I be | you be | he, she, it be | we be | they be |

Note that the use of the verb *be* in the present tense of the subjunctive mood is rather rare. In most cases it appears only in formal statements, or among the severely uneducated who don't know any better. Here's an example:

> The evil queen demanded that Snow White be banished from the kingdom.

In the subjunctive past tense, *be* is the only verb whose form differs from the indicative. The difference appears only with the singular pronouns *I*, *he*, *she*, and *it*. Thus, the form *were* is used for these subjunctive constructions, except when following the verbs *recommending*, *requiring*, or *requesting*. In these instances, *be* is used. This form of the subjunctive is frequently used to express a wish or make statements that are contrary to fact.

Indicative

I was   he, she, it was

Subjunctive

I were   he, she, it were

Here are some examples of this hardest of hard core grammar stuff:

> I wish the prince were here now. (Particularly note the use of *were* instead of *was*. *Were* is an example of the subjunctive form in use.)

> If I were in charge of making poisoned apples, you would see some major changes.

> The evil queen requested that all potions be sent to her first for approval.

As you can clearly see, trying to understand this higher concept of verb moods tends to put you in a mood of your own. And chances are that mood is not a pleasant one. But if you understand these three moods of verbs and use these forms correctly, you'll be one of the very few people who truly grasp one of the most technical aspects in grammar. True, there aren't many of you out there, but maybe you can start a yearly get-together and ramble on about subjunctive moods and tenses. Yeah, that should be a fun time had by all!

Chapter 15

tips to tip the grammar scale in your favor

Understanding grammar can be a true challenge, and unfortunately, even if you memorize every rule and grasp every concept, it doesn't guarantee that you're going to be a good writer or top-notch speaker. In fact, your words, no matter how grammatically sound they may be, can still put everyone to sleep. This may sound bizarre, but the same theory holds true in many other aspects of life as well. Just because you know every rule of football doesn't mean you can score a touchdown. Just because you know the rules of the road doesn't assure you that you won't be in an accident. And just because you know engineering doesn't mean you can figure out just how they get a damned boat to fit inside a thin-necked bottle.

But the truth is that even if you're a grammar expert, you can still be as dull as dirt. Why? Because you still may express yourself with dull constructions. Instead of communicating with sharp, clear ideas that paint distinct images in the minds of your listeners and readers, your words may be flat and your ideas may be fuzzy. It's like watching a grainy black and white TV instead of a high definition model that makes you almost feel you're a part of the action. Good analogy, huh? I thought so.

Most people appreciate listening to a good speaker, or reading the work of a talented writer who has the ability to express ideas as adeptly as an angry toddler expresses a tantrum. The words of such people are packed with meaning. You know what they're saying and you're left with a strong impression of their work.

While there are many things that people can do to capture the reader's attention, like using well thought-out ideas, precise words, and, of course, dirty language, there are three techniques in particular that can help you express yourself in ways that'll make your words and ideas apparent. These techniques focus on parallel structure, metaphorical images, and symbolism. Each of these three techniques can be a potent enhancement to your words (yes, I know it's not as much fun as using dirty language, but it can work just as well).

Parallel Structure

Parallel structure is the use of two or more elements in a sentence, or even sentences, to represent comparable ideas. Parallel structure can draw attention to ideas by reinforcing the similarities or differences between them, which thereby helps your audience to understand the ideas. Good speakers and writers often use parallel structure to add emphasis to their words. Once you're clear on what parallel structure is, you'll notice how often this technique is used. For instance, the great American patriot Patrick Henry uttered a famous statement that's an excellent example of parallel structure. In it, you'll notice that a specific repetition makes words stand out. In the example, the parallel structure is italicized.

> "I know not what course others may take, but as for me, *give me liberty or give me death*."

Although not many people remember the specific incident in which Henry said those words, most people do remember the last part of that famous statement. That's because the parallel structure fills those words with power and makes them hard to forget . . . especially when your history teacher drilled them into you like she was using a heavy-duty power tool.

Julius Caesar is another famous speaker and someone who was known for not mincing words. He too used the power of parallel structure when he said the immortal words:

> "I came, I saw, I conquered."

That sentence is clear and direct. It's memorable and has been remembered for over 2,000 years.

And let's not forget that bifocal inventor and kite-flying genius, Ben Franklin, who used parallel structure in summing up the American rebels' need for unity:

> "We must indeed all hang together, or, most assuredly, we shall all hang separately."

Okay, enough with the history lesson. Here are some examples of parallel structure that are far more current:

> "I laughed, I cried, it became a part of me."
>
> "The thrill of victory, the agony of defeat."

Even though these quotes may seem to flow effortlessly, there is a method to their madness. In order for parallel structure to be effective, it must be expressed in the same grammatical forms. You have to pair the same types of speech together—for example, nouns to nouns, adjective phrases to adjective phrases, or clauses to clauses. You also need to connect the ideas in the same types of ways. You can't just toss them together like a mixed green salad. You have to layer them carefully like a four cheese lasagna. (Can you tell it's time for me to break for lunch?)

Take a look at Caesar's quote, "I came, I saw, I conquered." Even though he was busy trying to lead an empire, he took the time to follow the specific pattern of words, in this case a pronoun verb, pronoun verb, pronoun verb. The sentence itself is made up of three clauses, all in the past tense. Grammatically and structurally, the statement is perfectly balanced. It's consistent, repetitious, and rhythmic. It's also clear, direct, and easy to recall. There's no ambiguity, no hesitation, no uncertainty. (Did any of you notice that I just used parallel structure? If you did, give yourself a little pat on the back.) Caesar's statement tells more than just a guy arriving somewhere, checking out the situation, and doing a little conquering. It paints the picture of a man who is confident and decisive, and will one day create the world's tastiest salad. (Man, I really do need to break for lunch.)

Although parallel structure is an effective tool in writing, if it's not used correctly, it can cause your sentence to become unclear, wordy, and grammatically incorrect. If this happens, you'll lose any impact the parallel structure might have otherwise had on the sentence. So be patient and take your time with it. If you thought parallel parking was tough, just wait till you try parallel structure.

Here's an example of an attempt to use parallel structure but it is used incorrectly.

You must always think clearly and act with honor.

Note that the verb and adverb "think clearly" are not similar in structure to the verb and prepositional phrase "act with honor." Although the sentence is correct, using a parallel structure makes it stronger.

You must always think clearly and act honorably.

In this example, the verb "think" and the adverb "clearly" parallel the verb "act" and the adverb "honorably." They make a stronger impression on readers or listeners.

But once you master it, you can use parallel structure in many different circumstances. One of the most common is the listing of ideas within a sentence, as in the following example I stole from a sign that hangs outside a local restaurant that has the most amazing blueberry pancakes:

"To satisfy our customers, we must be willing to listen to their concerns, we must be willing to act upon their concerns, and we must be willing to satisfy their concerns."

In the example, note how repetitive clauses, each of which ends with *their concerns*, are used to set up the parallel structure. This provides great clarity and emphasis. It adds punch to the sentence and stresses the point that the restaurant is trying to convey that satisfied customers are of paramount importance. But not nearly as important a selling point to me as those yummy pancakes.

You can also use parallel structure to compare or contrast ideas, as in the following:

Peter likes eating cakes more than he likes eating cookies.

In this example, *likes eating cakes* and *likes eating cookies*, which have the same structure, focus on the same ideas, namely, tasty baked treats. The meaning of the sentence therefore brings on sharp simplicity, as well as severe hunger pangs.

Parallel structure also works well with correlative constructions such as *both . . . and*, *either . . . or*, *neither . . . nor*, and *not only . . . but*. Here's an example of what I'm talking about:

Sarah not only makes bread dough but she also kneads bread dough.

In this example *makes bread dough* and *kneads bread dough* clearly indicate what Sarah does. The parallel structure makes it easy for the listener to focus on the main point of the sentence, or at least they would if they weren't distracted by their empty rumbling tummies, like mine.

It's not enough, however, to use the right grammatical forms and compatible ideas when you use parallel structure. You also have to make sure that your expression is clear. Using repetition is a good and effective way to help your audience follow along with your ideas and to see them through to their logical conclusion. When you repeat an article, a preposition, or even an entire phrase, it can give your words the extra punch they need. It's like adding Tabasco sauce to an otherwise plain meal of scrambled eggs. Sure the eggs are a perfectly acceptable dish without it, but hoo-boy, they sure have a memorable kick when you toss in a few dashes of that Tabasco stuff! Okay, that's it, I gotta go get something to eat!

Metaphors and Similes

Now that I'm back and my stomach is full, let's continue with the other ways to capture your audience's attention. Parallel structure isn't the only technique that can add flavor to a sentence. Another technique that you can use is called a metaphor. When you went to school, you learned that a metaphor is a figure of speech. You learned about similes and how they're a great way to make a comparison. And, of course, you learned that your crush will finally say hello to you on the same day you get a honking zit on your nose.

In case you forgot exactly what your teacher told you about metaphors and similes, let me take this opportunity to remind you. A simile is a comparison of two different ideas by way of the words *like*, *as*, or *than*. Here's an example of a simile, which demonstrates the current condition of my happy belly:

> When I am full, my stomach looks like pregnant Demi Moore in the infamous *Vanity Fair* cover.

A metaphor is a comparison too, but unlike a simile, it makes its comparison without using any of the signal words (*like*, *as*, or *than*). Metaphors are much more common than similes and are used far more often in everyday conversation. In fact, a lot of our daily and written language is metaphorical. Here are some examples of what metaphorical speech actually looks like:

> She almost drowned in her tears.
>
> Ted is a big bear of a man.
>
> The fog blanketed the coast.
>
> When the subject turned to baseball, Reggie turned into a book of statistics.

When speaking and writing, adding metaphors is a great way to add force and imagery to your words. Strong and obvious metaphors can paint colorful and detailed images in the minds of your audience. This in turn helps them understand the true meaning of what you're trying to get across. But when used incorrectly, metaphors can be a dangerous thing. Okay, maybe dangerous is a bit too strong of a word. They don't pose the danger of drugs, smoking, or crossing your eyes so long they stay that way. But you should still use caution.

To ensure that your metaphors only add and don't detract from your sentence, be careful that the ideas your metaphors are tying together are clear and logical and within the context of the sentence. Most importantly, they need to be grammatically compatible. If you ignore these guidelines, you run the risk of creating mixed metaphors, which can be downright silly and unclear. Here's an example of what can go wrong with a metaphor when it becomes somewhat exaggerated to make its point:

> After Wilson cooked up the new jingle for the ad campaign, his stock in the agency rose, and he was on top of the mountain.

As you can see, this is a perfect example of when less is more. Although a listener or a reader will be able to get the gist of the sentence, which is that Wilson obviously wrote a jingle that proved to be successful for advertising and his reputation subsequently rose, the sentence may be more memorable because of its mixed metaphors instead of Wilson's success. Also, take note of how cooking, stock, and the reference to a mountain top are used to describe Wilson's action and success. The links that tie them together are so weak that the sentence doesn't have much strength and directness. In addition, *cooked* is a verb, *stock* is a noun, and *on top* and *of the mountain* are prepositional phrases. It's a regular smorgasbord of grammar! All of this mishmash undermines any connection that your audience can draw from your ideas and makes your sentence as weak as a martini served at a low-budget wedding. Here's a possible revision:

> After Wilson wrote the new jingle for the ad campaign, his stock in the agency rose.

Although the revision may not be flashy, it's direct and clear and a huge improvement over the former. And it doesn't contain a lot of weak metaphors.

Granted, metaphors can fill your expressions with vivid imagery, but only if they are clear, crisp, and sharp. If not, they can be as disturbing as, well, say a pair of eyes that are crossed for a very long time. Take my advice and stay away from committing either offense.

Symbolism

Symbolism is a method of giving something a meaning that's greater than just itself. If you look around, you'll notice that symbolism is a part of your everyday life. In fact, symbols are all around us. A flag is a symbol of a country. A dove is a symbol of peace. And the letters XXX are a symbol of a place that you don't want your husband to frequent. A perfect example of symbolism is the sentence—He finally saw the light—which is about some guy who finally came to an understanding about something he's been struggling with.

Using symbols in your speaking and writing can help your audience understand your ideas much more quickly. It can also leave them with a distinct impression of your meaning. That is, of course, if your audience has a good grasp of the English language. If not, they'll tend to take your meaning literally, which, in the above example, will make them think you're talking about some guy that's been struggling to find the on/off switch.

Like parallel structure and metaphors, the most effective symbolism comes from sentences that are grammatically correct and that clearly link ideas. Here's a good example about a man who's taking over a business:

> You shouldn't look upon this day as a time when dusk settles on the land and the night looms ahead, but rather as a new dawn and a coming day filled with opportunity for all of us.

Here, the symbolism makes the meaning clear, and the sentence has substantial impact.

At the risk of sounding like a broken record (an example of a simile in case you missed it), I have to give the same strict warnings as I did with the other sentence enhancers. Although the use of symbols can add strength to your words, you must use them with a gentle hand (a metaphor showing that you need to exert caution). Overusing symbols tends to diminish their effectiveness and can come across as if you're padding your words with unnecessary material. Moreover, too many symbols can cloud your ideas and cloud your meaning (yes, that's an example of parallel structure. I think you're getting the hang of this stuff).

Even after you get the hang of this stuff, you can never underestimate the importance of proofreading. Here are some tips to make proofreading as painless as possible.

Better Ways to Proofread

In your typical conversation with your average gal-pal or boy-toy, you have a measure of grammatical laxity that you don't have in writing. For example, when you speak you don't need to italicize the title of a movie that you're talking about because your listener understands that you're talking about a movie.

But things aren't as easy when you're writing, for the written word reveals all of your flaws for the eye to see, like a heavy woman wearing a g-string bikini. This is why you have to work hard at perfecting your grammar skills so that your writing is free of grammatical faux pas. Once you hand your boss that crucial report that you've filled with mistakes, there's no taking it back (unless, of course, you happen to have a time machine, in which case, I'd appreciate it if you'd let me borrow it so that I can go back to 2002 and sell off my damn tech stock before the market plummets into the toilet).

I find that it's just as important to take the time to proofread your work as it is to know the rules of grammar in the first place. Proofreading is your last opportunity to put the final polish on your writing. It's the time that you can correct any grammar mistakes, fix any typos, and take out that "Dear Mr. Dick-wad" intro that you wrote when your boss pissed you off.

Proofreading may sound simple, but the truth is that if it's done correctly, it's no easy task. Sure, the large glaring mistakes are relatively easy to catch. It's the subtle ones, or the ones that come from just plain oversight, that you need to watch out for. When proofreading, you need to focus on every paragraph, every sentence, every word, and every punctuation mark. Effective proofreading requires that you

❝When I start typing I go really fast and don't pay much attention to spelling. I used to only change the mistakes that were caught by spell check, but I learned the hard way that they don't highlight words as long as they're spelled correctly. This was when my article was published in the school bulletin about the merits of my new Vulva station wagon.**❞**

—Andrea

draw upon all of your newfound grammatical power. If your idea of proofreading is simply giving your document a quick once-over like you do the directions for an assemble-it-yourself project, then you may be setting yourself up for failure. If you don't believe me, why don't you test out the strength of that side table you just put together.

The next time you proofread your material, here are some pointers you can use to help catch those subtle little devils:

1. Read slowly and concentrate on your writing. Look for mistakes in punctuation, capitalization, word usage, and, of course, spelling.
2. Check that each of your sentences flows as smoothly as twelve-year-old scotch. Be sure that it conveys just what you want to say. Imagine that you're naively reading your document for the first time.
3. Look at each page and make sure that all of your paragraphs are indented, your margins are correct and even, and that your words don't have any apparent gaps like the ones in David Letterman's front teeth.

4. If you're proofreading on a computer screen, use the cursor to move down through the text one line at a time. Avoid reading fast and scrolling or you'll be more likely to miss mistakes. And if you're one of those people who prefer to proofread printed pages instead of those on the screen, then by all means, print out your document first.

5. If you're using a grammar checker and spell checker, examine each flagged word and expression carefully. Make certain that any corrections you decide to make that are based on a checker's suggestions are in fact correct. Depending on the construction and the meaning of an expression, these computer checkers can sometimes be wrong. If in doubt, consult a reference book.

6. When proofreading, always have a dictionary and grammar book handy. When references are nearby, instead of on the high shelf like mine always are, you're more likely to use them.

7. And my own personal favorite: Try to read your document aloud. I find that I catch a lot of mistakes this way.

Below you'll find some guidelines of mistakes that you should be looking out for . . . in addition to that Dick-wad comment. In fact, you can tear out these pages and keep them in your wallet for quick reference. (Hey, if you're thinking that calling your boss a dick-wad is okay, then you need all the cheat sheets you can get your hands on.) In sum, when you're proofreading, be sure that:

1. The first word in a sentence, all proper nouns, and all proper adjectives are capitalized.

2. Sentences have correct ending punctuation: periods, question marks, and exclamation points.

3. Commas are used for lists, to set off phrases and clauses, in dates, between city and state, after direct address, to set off quotations, and after the closing of a letter.

4. Colons are used to set off a list, for time, and after the greeting of a business letter.

5. Semicolons are used to join independent clauses and for internal punctuation in lists.

6. Apostrophes are used to indicate possessive nouns and contractions.

7. Quotation marks are used for the titles of stories, songs, poems, the chapters of books, and to indicate the direct words of speakers.

8. Italics are used for the titles of books, plays, movies, TV shows, the names of newspapers and magazines, and the names of major vehicles of transportation.

9. Minor punctuation marks such as parentheses, dashes, ellipses, and slashes are used correctly.

10. The tenses of verbs are correct.

11. Spelling is correct.

12. Subjects and verbs agree.

13. Pronouns agree with their antecedents.

14. Unnecessary words and phrases have been eliminated or revised.

15. The meaning of each sentence is clear and expresses precisely what you wish to say.

Along with proofreading for mistakes in grammar, you should also look for any unnecessary words or phrases in your writing. Unnecessary material makes for clutter, which undermines the clarity of your work and makes it hard for your ideas to stand out. Written clutter is like wearing too many accessories with a busy outfit, or, in boy terms, it's like too many Hooter waitresses when you're trying to concentrate on the big game. Either way, it makes it harder for the audience to focus on what's important.

To help you avoid this unnecessary clutter, I'm going to give you a list of wordy and redundant phrases. Wordy phrases are those that contain more words than are needed to express ideas. For example, it's better to change *all of a sudden* to *suddenly*. Redundant phrases are those that repeat similar ideas, such as *basic fundamentals*. *Basic* and *fundamental* mean the same thing. In either case, whether wordy or redundant, these phrases should be eliminated or changed before your writing can be considered finished.

Wordy or Redundant Phrase	Revised
all of a sudden	suddenly
as a matter of fact	the fact is
as of this writing	yet
as to whether	whether
as yet	yet
at the present time	now
basic fundamentals	fundamentals
be in a position to	can
be kind enough	please
big in size	big
by means of	by
commute back and forth	commute
completely filled	filled

Wordy or Redundant Phrase	Revised
distant past	past
doctor by profession	doctor
due to the fact that	because
during the time that	while
each and every	every
end result	result
exactly the same	identical
exact replica	replica
extreme hazard	hazard
foreign imports	imports
for the purpose of	to
free gift	gift
in accordance with	by
in close proximity	nearby
in the near future	soon
in order to	to
in reference to	about
in regards to	as regards
in relation to	about
in the event that	if
in view of the fact	as
kindly arrange to send	please send
new record	record
none at all	none
on a few occasions	occasionally
on the subject of	about
order up	order

Wordy or Redundant Phrase	Revised
past history	past
personal friend	friend
postponed until later	postponed
prior to the start of	before
red in color	red
resulting effects	effects
return back	return
seems to be	is
serious danger	danger
still persists	persists
successfully completed	completed
ten in number	ten
that there	that
the honest truth	truth
this here	this
thought to himself	thought
totally destroyed	destroyed
totally unanimous	unanimous
under the circumstances	because
until such time	when
very unique	unique
whether or not	whether
with regard to	about
with the exception of	except

Now that I've taught you everything I know about proof-reading, let's see how much you know. Go ahead and take

a pass at proofreading the paragraph below and correcting
all of the mistakes. Although there may be differences with
writing styles, all of the mistakes below are universal ones.
Once you're finished proofreading, you can compare your
work with the corrected paragraph that follows. Good luck,
and don't forget to keep your eyes off your neighbor's paper.
Ready, go:

> People who speak well and write well have a significant advantage
> over the man who lacks the ability to express himself correctly and
> fluently. Effective communicators are often perceived to be more
> educated, more knowledgeable, and most competent then there col-
> leagues. They are often considered first for promotions and rise rap-
> idly through the ranks to assume positions of leadership. This should
> not hardly be a surprise. The man or woman whom is able to express
> themselves clearly is an asset to just about any company or organiza-
> tion.

> People who speak well and write well have a significant advantage
> over people who lack the ability to express themselves correctly and
> fluently. Effective communicators are often perceived to be more
> educated, more knowledgeable, and more competent than their col-
> leagues. They are often considered first for promotions and rise rap-
> idly through the ranks to assume positions of leadership. This should
> not be a surprise. The man or woman who is able to express himself
> or herself clearly is an asset to just about any company or organiza-
> tion.

Well? How'd you do? There were actually several things
you could have corrected. You might have corrected some
things in a slightly different way, depending on whether you
used plurals or singulars in your corrections. If you got them
all right, you can consider yourself head and shoulders above
the crowd. If you missed just one or two, then maybe you
should consider yourself just one shoulder. If you missed a
lot, well, then, consider yourself in need of reading this section over again.

Chapter 16

some final thoughts

As you know, time has brought with it a bounty of important changes. Horses and chariots have made way for automobiles. Writing tablets have made way for computers. And petticoats have made way for thongs. The English language is no exception and has changed dramatically over the years.

Changing Grammar in a Changing World

To prove my point, find a copy of Geoffrey Chaucer's *The Canterbury Tales* written in late fourteenth-century English. Though you'll recognize a few words, you'll probably have no idea what the heck they're trying to convey. They may as well have been written in Klingon, or Swahili for those of you who actually do speak Klingon. I know you're out there because I've dated many of you. Although Chaucer wrote this book in English, his English is vastly different from the English we're familiar with today. His book is tangible proof of how much our language has changed over the years.

Not only did it change, it changed quite fast. In fact, only some two hundred years after Chaucer wrote his book, educated English men and women were already having trouble understanding Chaucer's original words. Since that time, however, English has been relatively stable, and like Queen Elizabeth's hairstyle, it has hardly changed at all. The only exception to this has been the addition of new words and expressions that have come about from necessity. The reason that English has remained stable is simple, yet significant. In 1485, the first printing press began operation in England, and the first steps toward standardization of our language were taken.

The person responsible for this was a man by the name of William Caxton, who was one of England's first printers. Caxton wanted to print books that the largest number of people would understand, but he discovered that this was no easy task. At the time, there were more than two dozen regional dialects that were spoken throughout England, some of which were so distinct that an Englishman from one part of the country might have trouble understanding a fellow Englishman from another. Think Martha Stewart trying to understand Snoop Dogg. Same language, different dialects.

❝For a few years now I've been using the word fantango that I made up to describe something wonderful. I know it's not a real word, but I'm hoping that it catches on and it becomes part of the English language. That way, in case I never have any kids, I'll have left my mark on the world!❞

—Justin

Realizing that it would be silly to print different books in the various dialects, Caxton instead chose to print his books in the language that was mostly understood in and around London, which was England's largest city as well as its capital. In time, London's English became the chosen English for all written works and academics. As more and more writers and printers emerged, and more and more schools began using this form of English, it soon became the nation's standard. The modern form of English that Caxton popularized is the basis for today's English. Fascinating, huh?

Once the language became standardized, it also became very stable. Rules for grammar began to take hold, as did boredom in English classes. This is because (as we've already learned in part 2 of this book) the rules for English were based on the rules for Latin. Since Latin didn't have much in common with English, the rules had countless exceptions, and learning grammar became frustrating and difficult.

But printing for the masses ensured that these rules would become the pillars of grammar, and these pillars were built as strong as the Sears Tower. Even to this day, new words continue to be absorbed into the language, but English speakers throughout the world can understand each other, with the exceptions of Ozzie Osbourne, Keith Richards, and anyone discussing the various tax codes—all because of standardization.

Despite its stability, English continues to change. Most of the changes that have taken place during the past five hundred years center around vocabulary. For example, words like *thee* and *thou* fell out of use by the late 1700s, except among Quakers. In the 1920s, the word *lot* was only supposed to be used in regard to a parcel of land. Today it's used to mean a good amount of something, for example, *a lot of money*. The word *alright*, despite being considered nonstandard, often appears in print. The chances are good that one day it will be *all right* to use *alright* instead of *all right*. It may also be acceptable to use *ain't*, at least in some instances, but never around my grandma. *All together* may be merged with *altogether*, and *all ready* may simply become another meaning of *already*. Some experts believe that *whom* is headed for the obsolete bin along with our appendix and pinky toe and that split infinitives will no longer be a big no-no in the future. Not too long ago, people felt that it was wrong to end a sentence with a preposition. But today, it's as acceptable as putting your elbows on the table or showing your butt crack when you bend over to pick something up in your low-rise jeans.

A variety of forces cause English to change. Regional expressions, slang, words that are absorbed from other places, individual words that are put together and used as one, shortcuts in terminology and usage, and words created to name new things like megabyte and Botox all pressure standard English to change in a subtle yet unstoppable way. With so many people speaking English—and not all of them speaking it correctly—it can be hard to remember what's right, what's wrong, and what's new. Nonetheless, it's still important to speak and write correctly, especially when you're in a professional or formal setting, and of course, around my grandma.

Now that you've read this book, or at least skimmed through the parts that you needed to learn, you've acquired a reasonably solid understanding of English. And like any new muscle that you've developed, you don't want it to atrophy. And there are ways to prevent this from occurring. When you read, notice the way that authors use words. When you converse, listen to how words are being used. Also, try to read a newspaper each day, or a weekly magazine each week (I recommend *Star* because it's filled with lots of juicy stuff). Think of these tools as a Bowflex for your brain. Not only will reading keep you up-to-date and informed, but newspapers and magazines are usually among the first places that new words and expressions show up to alert you to changes in our language. If you're truly interested in maintaining your sharp grammar edge, visit Web sites that are devoted to grammar. Although Web sites come and go, a simple search using the key words "English language" or "English grammar" will offer many sites (well, maybe not as many as penile enhancement sites, but there will still be a lot to chose from).

Understanding Standard English and its grammar will help you to recognize the changes that naturally occur in our language. This, more than anything else, will help you keep your knowledge of grammar as sharp as a surgeon's laser. See? That's an example of one of those new words I talked about. The first actual laser was observed in 1960, and it took several more years for the word to make its way out of the laboratories and into the general language.

May the Force Be with You:
What You Can Do with Your Newfound Power

With your newfound understanding of grammar, you are now strong and masterful like a Jedi fighter. You have the power to speak in a confident manner. You have the ability to write in a correct style. This elevates you far above the many others who don't have grammatical ability. Knowing grammar enhances your stature socially and professionally. It compels others to treat you with respect. And it scores you a date with the dual-bunned Princess Leah. Well, maybe it won't do that, but it really can do the other things. With your grammatical skill at hand, people will look up to you as a person who's well educated. The mere fact that you have this knowledge that most others lack turns you into something that your parents always told you that you were—special.

As more and more good jobs are created in the business world, employers need to staff these positions with the best men and women that they can find. Without question, with all other qualifications being equal, the person who doesn't say things like, "I'm amongst the top of my class" and "I can't hardly wait to start," will have a far better chance at landing the job. That is, except for those jobs that require you to ask, "Paper or plastic?"

But remember one thing, young Skywalker: Never move over to the Dark Side. You should use your power for good, and never evil. While you may be tempted to do so, abstain from using your skills to correct the grammar of your colleagues, your coworkers, and especially your boss. Instead, you should use your knowledge wisely, to speak and write effectively, and with more clarity than you did before. This alone will draw positive attention, just as poor speaking and writing will draw negative attention. For instance, you can give a presentation or write a report that's filled with impressive facts and sound ideas, but if your grammar is weak, your material will be tarnished. It's like a gorgeous woman who happens to have a giant wart on her face. Sure, at first glance you'll be intrigued by her beauty, but it won't take long for you to notice her flaw, and soon that hideous ball of skin will be all you'll see.

Now that you've finished this book, think of this last paragraph as your graduation day. Go ahead, move that tassel to the left, and tell your dad to buy you a new car. Just like a diploma, this newfound knowledge of grammar is a great asset, as will be that new car, and both will take you far. Off to a galaxy far, far away in fact. Or at least to a more successful and lucrative life than the one you had before, when you thought a pronoun was someone who was for a noun. My best wishes to you as you move ahead in all the different aspects in your life! Live long and prosper! (Yes, I know that's from *Star Trek* and not *Star Wars*, but it works a hell of lot better than "There is a great disturbance in the Force.")

Index